DESIGN
&
DRAWING

An Applied Approach

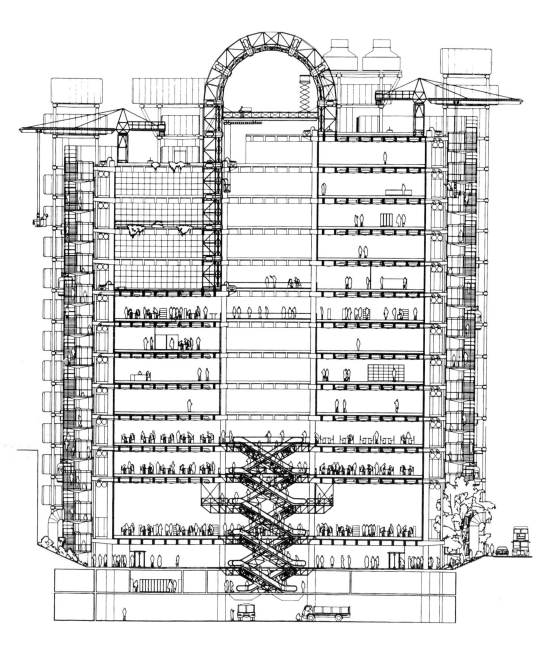

The Lloyd's of London office tower is a micro-community where people interact with each other and technology. Architects create these special environments for special activities. While a great building helps workers to achieve higher efficiency, it should also be a visually stimulating place. This drawing of the structure in section view shows the flow of space within the building. (Architecture: A Modern View, Richard Rogers, Thames and Hudson, 1990. Reprinted with permission)

DESIGN

&

DRAWING

An Applied Approach

Richard L. Shadrin

Davis Publications, Inc.
Worcester, Massachusetts

To Jan:
a test of faith rewarded...Thanks

About the author:
Rich Shadrin's dad was a typographer who taught him the beauty of a well-designed letterform, a nicely kerned headline and a clear paragraph with no wrong fonts. He holds degrees from the State University Colleges at Farmingdale and New Paltz, New York, and the School of Visual Arts. He is Director of Visual Arts for the Newburgh Enlarged City School District in New York State. A consultant to New York State Education Department, he also holds many awards in graphic design. He lives with his family in Walden, New York.

Printed in the United States of America
Library of Congress Catalog Card Number: 91-073901
ISBN: 0-87192-243-6

Interior Design & Composition: Greta D. Sibley
Cover Design: Paola Di Stephano
Illustrations: (id•e•o•blast) (de'•zin)

10 9 8 7 6 5 4 3 2 1

PREFACE

• Responsible design takes energy and vision. How do we tap the creativity resident in all of us. Is there a mysterious method to design? How do we nurture an idea into existence? This a detective story, and it's important to all of us who inhabit the built and designed environment. Although what we use is often what we tolerate, we would be better off in forsaking the role of complacent bystanders and learning about, and being critical of, the designed world. We must improve our design responsibility quotient.

• *Design & Drawing* explores the dynamics of the design process — from concept to product. There is a thrill in *designing* something that will be used and enjoyed by others. Through *drawing,* we can commit our free-floating ideas to a sheet of paper or a computer screen. Drawing is the essential link between creating and producing. It is how we get designs "out-there."

• This book originates from a syllabus for high school students in New York State called Design and Drawing for Production. This program recognizes the need for artists to understand technology and for

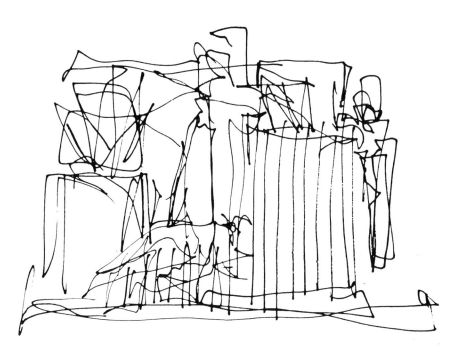

Preliminary sketch by Frank Gehry for American Center, Paris, France.

technologists to participate in the creative act. It's not that these qualities have been overlooked or undervalued by individuals, but that organizations of people have, in the past, neglected this most holistic of design truisms. *Design & Drawing* attempts to forge a stronger bond between art and technology.

RLS
September 1, 1991

CONTENTS

K A A

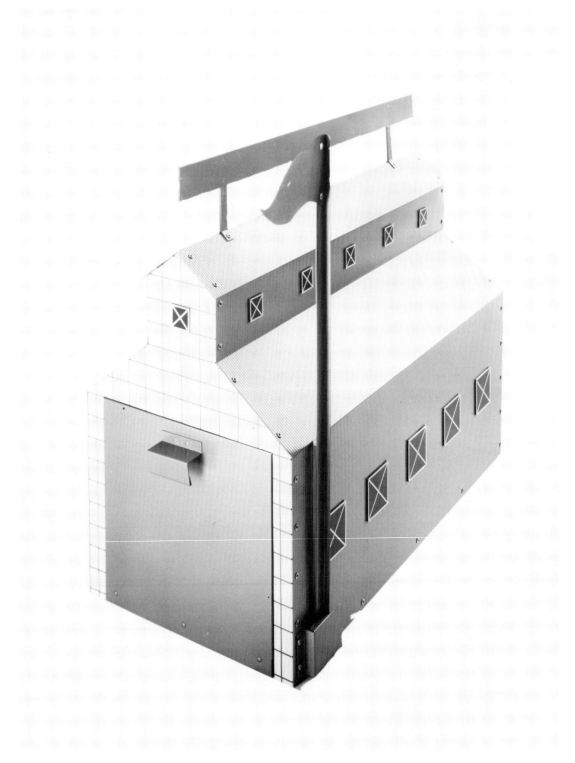

Architect Stanley Tigerman's mailbox design is a replica of his barn. Corrugated steel gives texture to the sides. (Courtesy of The Markuse Corporation)

INTRODUCTION

IS DESIGN PROBLEM–SOLVING?
IS PROBLEM–SOLVING DESIGN?

What is
THIS THING CALLED
design

Some people think design is something you do to solve a problem. Others feel that design is actually a mental process in which you think up ideas. It has been said that design is an act of creation and construction. Yet, I've read that it is an act of destruction, too! No wonder it is difficult to get a handle on this subject.

- First we need a basic understanding of the nature of design. Then we can clearly define it.
- Suppose you want to move a pile of broken tree limbs from your yard to the street for trash removal. The tree limbs are awkward. Twigs poke you and fall out when you try to carry them. You get an old sheet, throw the rubbish on it and drag it down to the curb.
- Have we designed something? No. Have we successfully solved a problem? Yes!
- Let's imagine that a sheet is not available. But in the garage are some pieces of wood, tools and nails. You use the tools to build a sled. Then you pile the twigs on the sled and pull them to the street.
- Because you consciously built a device to solve the problem, you not only did your chores — you participated in an act of design.
- This may not sound like much of a difference, but it is. Using a sheet shows a keen eye and common sense. These are two requirements of any design-doer. But building the sled involves thinking up a solution and then proving it by choosing the

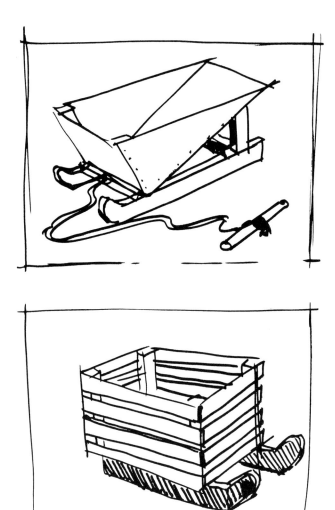

right material, figuring out a way to build it, laying out the parts to make a whole unit and showing that it can do the work.

- That is what design is all about.

Birth of the Twigster™

- Imagine you can't come up with an idea on your own. Where could you turn for an answer?
- You might look in a book of plans or talk to a neighbor who has had the same problem with twigs. If you're really intense, you could check out the encyclopedia or a textbook about architecture. In these books, you would find ways in which earlier civilizations solved the problem of moving objects, some quite large, from place to place long before anyone knew about the internal combustion engine, fluid dynamics and electromagnetic force.
- After thinking up a possible answer, you decide to share it with a friend. But he doesn't understand your idea. What can you do? You could draw the sled for him. When he sees the drawing, he offers a few comments on how he could make the sled better, or simpler, or better looking or... you get the idea. Friends are like that sometimes. But, in the spirit of friendship, he will help you build the object. Now there is another problem: he doesn't know how to turn your drawings into a real sled. You get help from your sister who can "read" plans and use the tools. And so your team builds the "TWIGSTER SLED."

- Then an amazing thing happens. Remember that neighbor? He still has twigs in his yard. Could you build him one of those sleds? Being the friendly sort, you say yes. But before you give him a price, you check out the cost of the wood and nails and, of course, pay yourself and your helpers. Pretty soon the whole village needs the TWIGSTER SLED and an industry is born.
- That's what this book is all about:

  ✔ identifying a problem,
  ✔ thinking up a solution,
  ✔ investigating other
    approaches to the solution,
  ✔ transferring the idea into
    drawings and
  ✔ figuring out how to build the
    idea or how to make it work.

GOOD DESIGN IS SPECIAL

- Good design is something quite special. A magnificent sunset can inspire great painting, falling in love, great poetry, allegiance to a flag, great music. So too can great design inspire strong emotion. Once in a while a design solution is just so good that people look at the object and react in unison: "Wow, is that great!"
- Notice the way musicians look at and handle a really well-made guitar or violin or saxophone. Or go to a car show and watch the faces of people around the low-slung sports cars. You'll know what I mean.

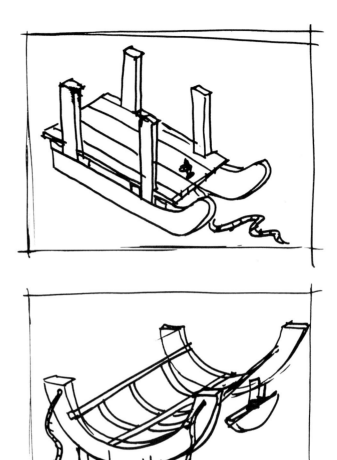

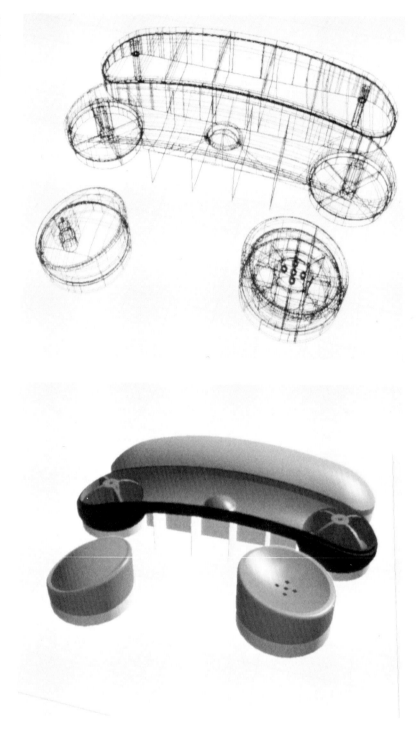

Computer-aided design systems shorten the product development cycle by months. Here is the birth of a new telephone receiver taking shape on a computer screen. (Courtesy of Design Continuum)

The search

FOR GREAT DESIGN

makes us explorers

in areas we wouldn't have imagined. Have you ever thought about the design of shoes? The "boating shoe," for example, is a classic design. It was intended to keep sailors from slipping on wet decks. Not only does the boating shoe do this brilliantly, it is also comfortable and, to many people, really good looking.

WHY BRAND X MIGHT BE BETTER THAN BRAND Y

• It is important that a product does its job well. Function is a critical element. To be successful, a product must be useful, dependable and attractive. However, many brand names are very similar; they all fit the bill. But buyers prefer one.

• Why?

• It is true some manufacturers design and build a product that performs better (or lasts better, or fits better). But the issue of style comes into play. How stuff is made into things is engineering. Making things more enjoyable and attractive to people is design. Design is a visual and tactile practice that results in a physical object having "style."

• For example: Does a gold watch keep better time than a plastic one? Not necessarily. Then why do people buy the expensive watch when they can get one that works just as well for hundreds of dollars less? Why do women totter around in high heels and men scrunch their toes in pointy little designer shoes when both could easily get comfortable footwear?

• This is where psychology, sociology and design all get mixed up together.

Boating shoes: From a nautical necessity to a fashion statement. (Courtesy of Docksides)

Sending out a message

• When we choose which stereo to buy, which shirt to wear, which wallpaper to hang on our walls, we send out a message. People tell a story about themselves, seek status or a sense of their own importance and success. Who we are is reflected by what we choose.

• When people see an expensive watch on somebody's wrist, they see that person as rich and powerful. (At least, that is what the wearer hopes. Some people might see a salesperson. Wearing prestige can backfire, you know.) When a person wears a multi-function digital watch, one with timers, alarms and a calculator/phone dialer, we assume something quite different. Here, we think, is someone who loves technology so much that he or she doesn't mind wearing a watch as big as a breadbox.

• The style choices we make in our daily lives, from the unremarkable (What socks will I wear with those slacks?) to the substantial (What automobile will I buy?) say something about us to ourselves and others. Of course, some decisions will always be based on price or function. When a surgeon is cutting you open end to end, he doesn't wonder what the particular brand of scalpel says about him. (At least, you hope not.)

• Still, we should understand that appearances play a giant role in our consumer society. After all, why buy a pair of sneakers when triple-soled, double-cushioned GoreTex-lined athletic shoes not only perform better, but look cool, too?

• Earlier, I used the example of the boating shoe. Look around you. You'll notice many people who never go near water, wearing different brands of these moccasins. The boating shoe has grown beyond its immediate purpose as a seagoing necessity. It has become a fashion statement.

Both watches tell time — and accurately, too. It's prestige and style — what the object says about the owner that often makes a designed object desirable. (Courtesy of Swatch and Seiko)

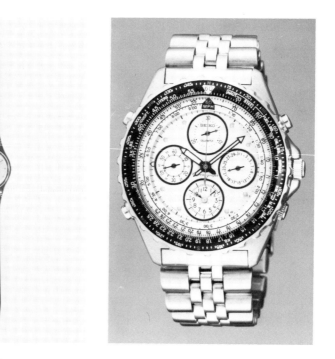

SIGN LANGUAGE

• Not too long ago, we were a print culture. That means people would read and write to get messages to each other. In a print society, newspaper articles and books are long and contain **COMPLEX** ideas. In our television dominated society we have become an image - based culture. We can rapidly communicate a feeling or an idea almost spontaneously through pictures.

• The American Indian used to send up smoke signals —their messages were, I'm sure, brief but **POWERFUL.** One set of puffs could declare war. Video images are short like smoke signals and they are more powerful yet. One brief image of a sunset over a beach can set up many, many **INVITING** thoughts.

• On a personal level, we use visual imagery every day. Our hands are the physical tools of formal and informal communication. What is a wave "hello" or "bye-bye" but a **SIGNAL.** What is "OK" and "thumbs-up"? Ask a Texan about "hook 'em Horns".

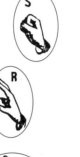

• Describe and create five new hand signs that are **INSTANT** representations of ideas, feelings, actions, places, **THINGS.** How would you signal "I'm going home now," or "Meet you at the mall?" Can you make up a signal that sends a message like, "I'm a cheerleader," "I'm a police officer," or "I herd sheep?"

• For reference, look at the signals workers use on a construction site when they are directing heavy equipment. You might also observe American sign language, the hand language used by the hearing impaired.

• If you can't draw hands well, use collage, or **POLAROID** photographs or video to explain your **SIGNS** to classmates, family or enemies.

A TOASTER IS A TOASTER IS A TOASTER

- Design is not haphazard or accidental. A designed object has meaning. Like fine art, a radio or toaster or skateboard is designed to spark an emotional or intellectual reaction in the viewer or user.

Are we buying hair dryers or ideas?

- Think about the look of home appliances and electronic equipment. They used to be chrome and white, with smooth, shiny finishes and rounded shapes. Now, the sharpest look in kitchen and home entertainment equipment is monotone. This means that one color or value dominates. There are no more shiny, painted surfaces. Textures are more important. Also, you might notice that the edges are sharp, the controls are laid out in groups and there is a feeling of sleekness.

- This is the "eurostyle" look. It reduces unnecessary detail: there are no frivolous parts, no extra curves. A sleek black stereo is no-nonsense, businesslike, high-tech. The person owning such a device must be those things too. Many new de-

This kitchen's surfaces are smooth, unbroken, flat and very industrial. It's a food-preparation laboratory. (Courtesy of KitchenAid)

Well-designed components make the operation of this stereo a tactile as well as a visual and aural thrill. (Courtesy of Proton Corp.)

vices use international symbols on their controls. This makes them easy to understand, no matter what language the owner speaks. It also makes the owner feel international.

• Coffeemakers, stereos and hair dryers are not just things we put in our home interiors. They *are* our home interiors. Since modern life demands that we surround ourselves with a lot of implements, tools, devices and appliances, these things have become a form of decoration. Every time we buy a designed object, we buy its meaning too.

The social meaning of architecture

• Giving meaning to things is not limited to individuals. Whole communities take part in design choices. When a village, town or city decides to put up a building, the form or design of the structure tells a story to the entire community. And if architecture is the art we all must live with, then we all should be able to influence it.

Newburgh builds a school

• In the early 1930s the city fathers in Newburgh, New York, realized that the town needed a new high school. They chose a firm of architects who specialized in education projects. Since the site for the new school was large and easy to build on, the actual design could take any shape or form. What style would best suit a school for this town?

• Well, the Newburgh area was

headquarters to George Washington and the Revolutionary War was discussed a lot in history classes. It had started as a farming community and it grew as the nation grew. Newburgh thought of itself as a very American city.

• Following this line of thought, the architects looked for examples of buildings inspired by two other great democracies — ancient Greece and Rome. Also, they reasoned, these two civilizations had placed great value on education.

• The unique architectural elements used by Greco-Roman designers have come down to us through actual style books and plans as well as standing ruins. The columns, arches, pediments, cornices and general proportions that the ancients used could be put together in a modern way.

• And so the school board was

The Parthenon (Athens, Greece, 447 BC) versus the Newburgh Free Academy Facade. Look at the elements in each facade. How has the old been reinterpreted to give meaning to the newer structure? (Courtesy of The Metropolitan Museum of Art, Levi Hale Willard Bequest, Purchase 1890; and Newburgh Free Academy)

presented with a sketch for the facade, or front elevation of the new high school. That it looked like a Roman temple or senate chamber should not surprise anyone. The community said, "We value education, for our children will be the leaders of the future. Let us build a structure that tells the world that, in this city, the government declares that education is important in order that our children can believe in and practice democracy."

• Schools, you see, are not just a place; they are also an idea. All buildings have meaning, the better ones more, the poorly designed less.

DESIGN ALWAYS HAS AN AUDIENCE

• Design never takes place in a void. Artists, painters, sculptors and photographers can often ignore their audience. They can challenge the public to guess or find meaning in their work. Designers always work in public because their designs generally result in practical use. And before pleasing the public, there is pleasing the client.

Designing logos

• Probably the greatest test of a designer's ability to communicate meaning is in the creation of logos. When a company wants to put its mark on a product, a graphic de-

1889

1900

1921

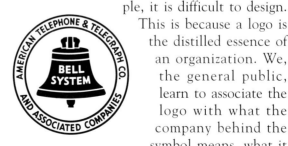

1939

signer creates a logo. That small symbol sends out two messages:

• One obviously tells us who made the product. But the other message tells us about the company itself.

• Since the symbol must be simple (because it is used in many ways, from business cards to signs on trucks) that little mark has to communicate a very big message. Throughout this century, these symbols have been pared down to very basic shapes. Even long established marks like RCA and AT&T have been simplified. Look at a new AT&T logo vs an old one: you will see how they reduced the details in the symbol.

• Although a logo is simple, it is difficult to design. This is because a logo is the distilled essence of an organization. We, the general public, learn to associate the logo with what the company behind the symbol means, what it

1964

1969

does, stands for, produces. These symbols become a communication shorthand, just like traffic signs. When we see them, we instantly understand the meaning behind the symbol.

The CBS eye

• For example, when we see the CBS "eye," we know it is the representation of seeing, but a special type of seeing. It is a television network, a visual communications business. But the company has a rich history, and therefore the logo does too.

• When we see the CBS eye, we automatically think of the shows on the network, some personalities too. Maybe you think of Connie Chung. Your parents might remember the great tradition of the news division and Walter Cronkite. Furthermore, we know that this is a big organization, very wealthy, employing thousands of people all around the world. When you pause a moment, it is really amazing — all that information from two small black shapes!

Reims Cathedral, begun in 1211, is a Gothic masterwork. Compare it to the simplicity of the seventh century Kamosu shrine in Japan.

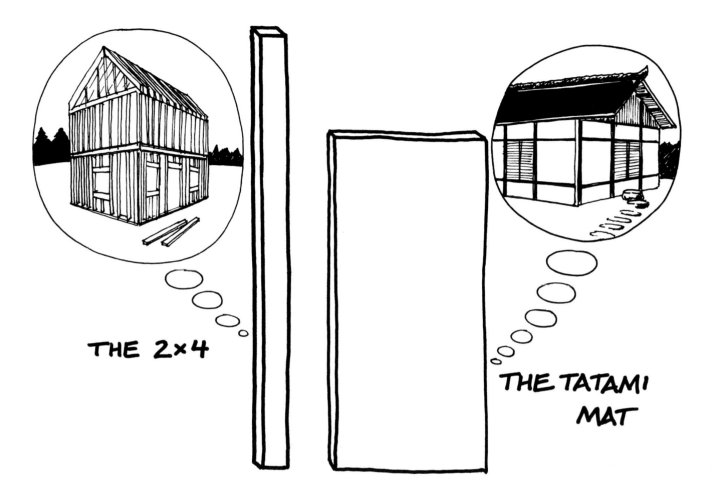

THE 2×4

THE TATAMI MAT

WHO YOU ARE AND WHERE YOU'RE FROM MAKES IT UNIQUE

• Design is affected by geography and culture. There is a world of difference between great buildings in the western world, such as the Parthenon or the Cathedral at Reims, France, and great Asian architecture, such as the Kamosu Shrine in Japan. Both the cathedral and the shrine are places of worship, but look at the difference in form and materials.

Materials

• You must realize that none of the choices the architect-builders made were casual. Even the materials available can determine the shape of a building. In Japan, for example, the tatami, or floor mat, measuring three feet by six feet, is the standard by which rooms are laid out. Closer to home, suburban houses are generally built based on western or balloon framing. The

Our culture as defined by the vehicles we use or desire... And those of the previous generations. Is it just technology that changes, or is it values? It's a design question as well as a social one. (Courtesy of Mazda and The Henry Ford Museum)

standard length and width of the structural lumber (2 x 4 x 8, etc.) determines the proportions and size of these houses.

Social Values

• Each culture, in its own way, seeks harmony. Where a Western architect might talk about the golden mean (perfect mathematical proportion), an Eastern architect might instead speak of "feng shui" (the harmonious placement of objects).

• The values we hold are reflected in the design of our important objects. Religion, race, wealth (or the lack of it), occupation, whether we live in the city or the country — all determine what we value. In turn, these values influence the objects we wear, use, travel in, shelter. The times we live in are important, too. The Walkman radio, Swatch watches, Nikes, Macintosh computers, the BMW, all are accepted as important objects of our time, just as bell-bottom jeans, peace symbols and psychedelic art were typical of the 1960s. Sure, the technology makes them possible, but people give them value as status goods. It is important for designers to understand this.

Is design becoming universal?

• An interesting point: Designers and artists fear that as the world grows smaller and new ideas travel at the speed of the electron, all designs will soon become universal. Objects for use in Bangkok will be the same objects for use in Chicago. Things will no longer have cultural or historical importance. Look at the skylines of Hong Kong (China), Edmonton (Alberta, Canada), Atlanta (Georgia, USA) and Rio De Janiero (Brazil). Not much different, are they?

Almost interchangeable aren't they? Why has this happened? (Courtesy of Boston Office of Travel and Tourism, and Dallas Convention and Tourism Bureau)

Sleek and dynamic, this clay car mock-up looks like it's moving even when standing still. (Courtesy of GM)

WHO DESIGNS?

• Design is not just one isolated act. It is a process with a beginning, a middle and an end. Throughout this book, both of us, author and reader, will have to wear two hats — designer and consumer — at the same time. That way, we can look at design from every angle.

• Why are some designs good and others not so good? Why do some buildings, products, even simple graphics excite the spirit and tingle the spine? To understand this, we'll have to examine first how these designs came into being and then why they work on us the way they do. The more we know about design, the more sensitive we become to it.

CAN DESIGN BE TAUGHT?

• Design has the capacity to reveal, attract and engage human thought and emotion. Yet, there is no magic at work here. Once you understand the basics of design, you can, on a reasonably steady basis, create poetry in everyday things. There are guidelines and signposts you can use to help answer a need or complete a project. But the shape that road takes and the smoothness of the journey depends a lot on you.

• The ability to analyze a problem, understand the purpose, know the audience, be aware of materi-

als, have skill in graphic communication, get passionate about ideas, receive and give critical feedback — these are all teachable things. The designer must bring curiosity, imagination, observation, guts and determination to the process.

• The challenge is great but the reward is greater. You can see something you created being used and admired. Very powerful medicine.

Shaker furniture is simple and direct, but very clever in it's construction.

Where the safety of a child is concerned, there can be no error in the designer's handling of function and form. (Courtesy of Rhode Gear)

When you start THE PROCESS OF designing,

you have to consider two primary factors: function and form.

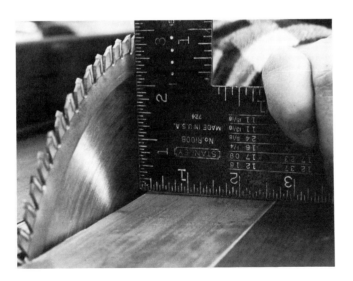

FUNCTION AND FORM

• Function is what you want the object to do. What is its purpose? What kind of work will it perform? Form is the physical quality of the object — the look and feel of it. How an object looks tells a story about it. This function/form combination is the reason why design, especially good design, is a marriage between science and art; technology and humanism.

• To be a successful designer you must have a clear picture of the task and the ability to find a solution that works. Then you have to communicate this solution to others through sketching, drawing, rendering and model-making so everyone can admire your brilliance.

Understanding the design problem

• First, you need to think about the function of the object. To start, you might ask yourself the following questions:

Considering function

✔ *What does it do ?* A tool, a building, a symbol, an appliance, a rug, each has a special function. You must clearly and completely understand what that function is.

Explain the function of this tool, without giving it a name — you'll understand why it looks the way it does. (Photo by Bill Byers)

This monster has the
same job as the table
saw. It's a tunneling
machine designed to cut
through rock. (Courtesy
of CP Rail)

✔ *How does it work?* Does it need a power source? A rug is not power driven; a table saw is. How does the need for power shape the appearance of the circular saw?

✔ *Who will use the object?* You know, the video tape recorder is in over 50% of all American households, but very few adults can program

theirs. (That little green clock does make a great night-light.)

✔ *Where will it be used?* This is critical. Designs for the same object will look very different if it will be used in the kitchen (near water), or in a machine shop (dirty, oily), indoors or outdoors, in the city, by the ocean and so on.

DOG HOUSE

We like to think that where and in what we live tells something about us. Given a choice, most people would live in an apartment or a house that was important and special. Throughout history, architectural styles have been and continue to be, the expression of this basic human desire.

But what about other species with whom we share our lives? Consider the dog. A friend, companion, pal, one of the family, one who has to share your home. Maybe they would like places of their own. Choose an architectural style from any time period expressed in a major residential building. Create a residence for a dog that would fit alongside that building.

Maybe your famous home is the Medici Palace (by Michelozzo), which set the standard for fifteenth-century princely places in Florence, Italy. What process would you use to translate that design into a miniature doggy version? Look at materials, details, the proportions of the building and other features like windows and doors. Since this structure was made of heavy stone and had a flat roof and rounded, arched window cornices, your Palazzo de Poodle might have the same.

If you chose instead an apartment in Barcelona in Gaudi's Casa Battllo, your dalmatian domicile would be completely different. Frank Gehry's home in Santa Monica, on the other hand, would have a very unusual deconstructivist canine domain.

Research, a keen eye for detail and a sense of overall shape and volume will assist you in answering this design challenge. And a sense of humor won't hurt, either.

A Frank Gehry-designed house in Venice, California, typical of his style.

Considering form

- Those four basic questions help you focus on the function of the task. At the same time, you need to think about aesthetic or appearance concerns, such as:

✔ *What competition will this product or object face?* This "competitive environment" idea is crucial. If you are to get your solution noticed, appreciated and in most cases, purchased, you have to take the competition into account. Perfume, for example, is a very competitive market. Go to a drug store or department store and look at all the perfume containers on the shelf. Notice how dramatic the containers are. What makes different ones stand out?

✔ *What type of client will the object attract?* If you are designing an object that everyone buys, your concept will be different than if it is just for left-handed people, athletes or millionaires. Certain people have expectations of quality or uniqueness or luxury; others need to feel a piece is technologically sophisticated. Some will use the object for work, as a tool, so they expect "performance-driven" design.

A.

Not a weird burger-flipper, but a surgical tool that holds back (retracts) the scapula ("shoulder blade") during surgery. (Courtesy of Codman and Shurtleff, Inc.)

PUTTING ALL THE CONSIDERATIONS TOGETHER

- Most often, all these considerations are important. You must learn to slow down your thinking so you can deal with every aspect of the problem. When a design solution is done right, it often merges great practicality and terrific looks.

Surgery tools

- Some really neat examples are tools for surgery — where human flesh meets steel! Thinking back over our list of considerations, you can see how surgery tools must be:

✔ Well-balanced (*Oops! Lost another scalpel in there!*),
✔ Ergonomically correct (*Is your hand getting tired, Dr.? That's okay, nurse, I'll just switch to my left hand and go on with this brain operation*), and
✔ Able to be sterilized. (*Let's forget that uncomfortable steel table. Put patient Jones over there on the sofa for his triple bypass.*).

- Most surgery tools are designed to do one task extremely well. These instruments are completely functional, appropriate to the user and the work. At the same time, they are intriguing designs.

• Yet another example is the public library. It is a building with a singular purpose — to store information that can be easily retrieved by the public. It should be user-friendly, accessible and inviting. But it should also be inspiring: a temple of knowledge. The best libraries not only invite you to use them, they also make you feel that you are in an important building.

GETTING STARTED

• With all these things to think about, it is often difficult to get started on a solution to a problem, let alone remember all the other important aspects of design, like historical reference points, drawing and model-making. It is a good thing that a system has evolved to help see inside a problem, research solutions, create answers, communicate those answers to others and ultimately get the object made or built. In the following chapters, we'll show you how this system works and give you examples, too.

• The system acts as a path to our goal. We all know, however, that some roads are straight and flat encouraging the traveler to speed directly to his destination. Some roads are two-lane jobs, inviting the traveler to observe the countryside at a more leisurely pace, pausing to take in some sights. And, finally, we have meandering lanes, winding their way over hills and around curves, pleasantly surprising the traveler with fresh vistas after every turn and dip.

Single objects vs. mass-produced

• One last thing, however. We've been talking about design objects as if everything a designer does results in 50,000 pieces rolling off an assembly line. While the mass-produced, high-tech product is a result of certain types of design, the low-tech, one-of-a-kind, hand-crafted object is a result of design as well. A design for sports sunglasses or a low-cost hairdryer must be good enough to sell in a market crowded with competitors. But a design for a single set of ceramic dinnerware, a handknit sweater or a custom-built set of golf clubs should be just as good.

Mass production versus hand-crafted objects. On an auto assembly line — large numbers of the same product require great standardization of parts...But, in one-of-a-kind production, the artist has great freedom of personal expression. Can the two ideas ever come together? (Courtesy of Jervis B. Webb Co. and Alice Sprintzen)

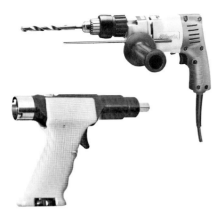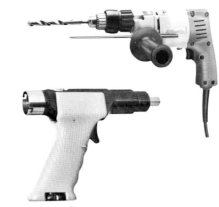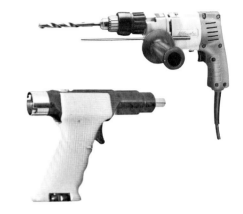

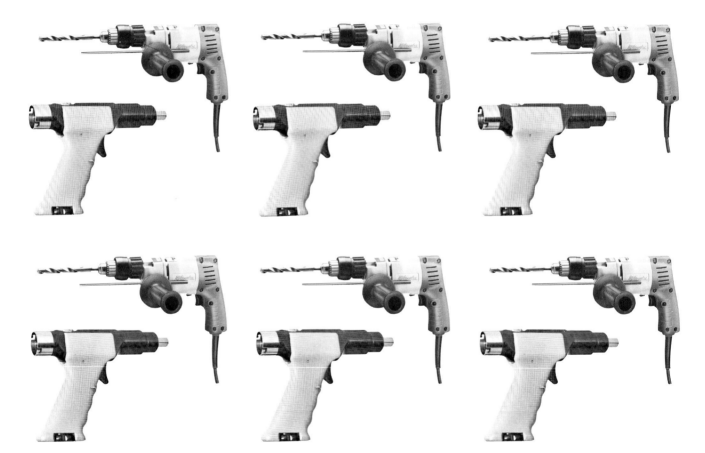

Craniotome versus a power drill. Similar, yes, but you can't practice brain surgery unless you can master the craniotome. It spins at 20,000 rpm, is powered by dry nitrogen and won't leave any bone chips in your head. (Courtesy of Codman and Shurtleff, Inc. and Milwaukee Electric Tool Corp.)

Milton Glaser
(1 9 2 9 -)

• Although trained as a graphic designer, Milton Glaser has designed many things — from typefaces and publications to furniture, jewelry, supermarkets and restaurants. His first entry into design beyond graphics was in 1972 when he created a flagship store in New York City for Childcraft,

Glaser's popular logo for New York has spawned many imitations.

the toy company. Soon after, he redesigned the Grand Union supermarkets. He created a new logotype, store signage, displays, the floor plan, even the exterior. The new look revived the business of the supermarket chain.

• An example of his talent is his work on the observation deck of the World Trade Center. To help visitors identify other buildings, Glaser outlined the shape of the building or site on the window glass. As you look through the glass at the Manhattan panorama, you can easily identify the important sites without having to turn away and look at a map.

An unforgettable Bob Dylan in poster form, by Milton Glaser. (Courtesy of Milton Glaser, Inc.)

Thomas Edison spent his entire life discovering and solving problems. Here he listens to an advanced model of one of his inventions: the phonograph. Does he seem pleased with his work? (Courtesy of The Henry Ford Museum)

To solve problems **creatively**

— WHICH IS OUR PURPOSE HERE —

we'll use seven categories

to organize our thinking and doing. We'll call these categories "constants." Every activity in design fits neatly into one or another.

• As you experience the design process, most often you'll be scurrying back and forth, using stuff from one constant, linking it to another.

Another one of Edison's solutions: the light bulb. It has become synonymous with good ideas. (Courtesy of The Henry Ford Museum)

Then maybe it will change some other thing, so you'll back up to take two leaps forward and so on. Because design is as much re-discovery as invention, these travels often result in happy accidents that make your solution much better.

• But happy accidents don't happen by themselves. Behind them is a lot of work and skill. There's an old saying about that: "Chance favors the prepared mind." (Louis Pasteur)

Solving a design problem directly ...very rare.

The usual agony.

THE SEVEN CONSTANTS

- The seven constants are:
  - ✔ Design Activity (*What is the problem?*)
  - ✔ Analysis (*What is the purpose and function of the design?*)
  - ✔ Historical Reference (*How was it done before?*)
  - ✔ Visual Communication (*How can I communicate my idea?*)
  - ✔ Skills (*What skills do I need for this design?*)
  - ✔ Technology (*How will the design or product be made?*)
  - ✔ Evaluation (*Is this the best solution I can come up with?*)

The Design Activity

- Here the problem is given to you, or someone states it. Or maybe you suddenly look up and realize that a need exists and so you set out to answer it. Sometimes a teacher gives you a task, a client has a problem or you just want to invent or design something that excites you.
- But remember: it's not enough just to receive the problem. You have to understand the nature of it as well. A simple sentence stating the problem often hides as much as it reveals. To uncover the hidden meaning, a designer must be a detective as well as an artist.

Analysis

- It is useless to stumble blindly into a problem with inadequate information. Artists and designers must gather as many ideas as possible. Then they apply those that fit and toss out those that just don't make it. Often a great answer comes from joining together bits and pieces of many ho-hum ideas.
- But it is hard to think up a lot of different possible solutions. There is a special strategy to help develop many diverse ideas. It is called brainstorming and it will be discussed later.

Historical Reference

• A good designer recognizes past solutions to similar problems. Many design students run for cover when they think they'll be spending hours in a library. Sometimes, yes, formal research is important. So it doesn't hurt to learn how to use reference material: books, pictures, plans, etc. But you can also look at popular sources, like television, fashion, music and language. The times we live in are full of ideas for a designer.

Visual Communication

• You have a great solution. Maybe it's even brilliant. But if you can't get it out of your head and onto a piece of paper, your idea is doomed. Design is visual creative problem-solving and drawing communicates that design. Every designer is an artist who communicates visually — from the roughest sketch to the most elegant rendering. All aspiring designers have to know all six types of technical drawing. That way they can tell other designers, manufacturers, builders and clients all about their brilliant ideas.

Skills

• Each type of drawing has unique features and special rules called *conventions*. Also, good storytelling means that an artist/designer must be familiar with a lot of different tools, from crayons to computers. You must also understand the elements of design and

A group discussion on solving design problems encourages students and teachers to stretch out towards unique answers.

principles of art. You, the designer, often have to convince someone else that your solution is the right one. How successful you are depends on your skills in using the tools.

Technology

• A designer must understand the relationship between the designed object and the production process. How will your product be made? Even if you've designed a one-of-a-kind handcrafted object, you have to know what materials and processes will go into making it. Quite often, you'll know from the very beginning what materials have to be used. Sometimes though, it's only when you have an answer that you start looking for the right

materials and manufacturing processes to bring your design to life.

Evaluation

• During the creative process, designers constantly question the "rightness" of what they are attempting. The formation of a project takes many decisions. Often what you choose to leave out is just as important as what you put in. It is necessary for you to become your own critic during your design activity.

• But don't forget: design is a public art form. Others will have something to say, too.

• The best way to prepare for their comments is to ask yourself the same questions first: Why doesn't it look like our older

DESIGN
Challenge

WHAT'S INSIDE?

Being curious by nature is a characteristic of a good designer. If you look up the word you'll find it means: *questioning, probing, prying,* and also *unexplored, unexpected* and, my favorite, *mysterious*. Since most of our discussion in this book turns on why things look the way they do, it is important to step back, or rather in, to see what goes on inside instruments, devices and machines.

A while ago, a designer friend of mine told me about a crazy collection he had started. Every time an appliance, tool, gauge and instrument breaks down beyond repair, he asks the owner or shop to donate it. He then brings it into his studio and takes it apart. In one corner of the studio there is a morgue of parts of refrigerators, hand mixers, dial faces and little bits and pieces.

Once you take the cover off something, he says, it is amazing what you'll find inside. I looked around and was fascinated—but curious too. So when my wife's electric mixer burned out, I took it into the garage for an autopsy. Before I opened it up, I tried to imagine what was inside. I

took note of the power cord, the switches and the receiving holes for the blades. How did the motor make the blades turn? What supported the motor and wires? What made the blades pop off? I created a mental image of what I'd find and then removed the six screws. It was so ridiculously simple that I actually laughed aloud. I thought, how we've all been taken in by these machines.

Start a collection of your own by visiting appliance dealers, repair shops, garages. Look at devices like springs, levers and gears, which are based on ancient principles and can be found in almost every product that seems complex. Identify as many simple machines as you can.

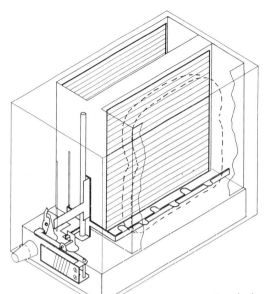

Even the thermostat in a toaster is a primitive computer. The more time is needed to move the contact arm, the darker the toast.

model? Why wood? How come it looks like a porcupine? Why is it yellow? What is its meaning? Why do I feel good when I pick it up?

• While you ask these questions, you have to keep in mind the difference between evaluation (*Does this solution work?*) and judgement (*Do I personally like it?*).

APPLYING THE DESIGN CONSTANTS

• By using the seven constants, you can tackle your design problems in a logical way without destroying the energy, imagination and innovation you need to be creative.

Another turn on the Twigster Sled

• Let's go back to the very first example — the "Twigster Sled." and apply the seven constants to the problem. The design problem, you'll recall, was to move a pile of twigs and sticks from your yard to the street. An important characteristic was the awkward nature of the material, which made the load bulky and unstable.

The first constant: The design activity

• If you were to write down the design problem, it might look like this:

```
A person has to
remove twigs from his
yard to the street.
The material is
thin, relatively light,
```

but hard to carry. Since the person does not want to make frequent trips back and forth, a method or device should be created to do this job.

• This is the statement for the design activity, the beginning of what all designers call a "design brief." When you look at a "brief" statement, make a list of the important points and then a list of what the brief doesn't say — things left out that could be important. For example, the statement reads: *A person wants to move material.* Well, you can list one person, but you can also list *only* one person.

• Get the difference?

• If only one person will pull the sled, we certainly shouldn't design it to carry a ton of material. On the other hand, we don't want to make it tiny, or the person will be going back and forth too much. (Not too many trips is another requirement of the statement.)

The second constant: Analysis

• When designers approach any problem, they "brainstorm" it. That means they explore many possible answers or parts of answers. We know that the Twigster Sled must carry material over two types of surface: grass and pavement. It has to be light when empty, manageable by one person when full. We can't use exotic materials because it will be manufactured locally.

Henry Dreyfuss
(American, 1904–1972)

• Dreyfuss was responsible for one of the most popular designs of the 1950s — the Bell telephone model 500. This jet black, bakelite, rotary dial telephone is now a classic. It is an excellent example of a commercial object streamlined and made to fit the human hand. Dreyfuss believed in designing for people. He developed systems for integrating the needs of the body with the tools people must use. He designed interiors for airplanes, ships and even farm equipment.

There are still some of the Model 500 telephones around.

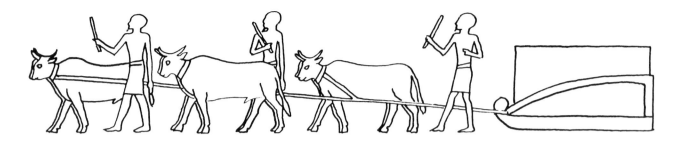

The Egyptian sledge moved heavy building stones over sand. The Portland Cutter sleigh (opposite page) moved people over snow. The principles are the same — just adapted for local conditions.

The third constant: Historical reference

• We also could do some historical research by looking in architectural texts and encyclopedias for other devices people have made to haul materials. If we really look hard, we will find a lot — from chunky Egyptian sledges moving stone blocks to the pyramids to elegant colonial sleighs skimming on runners over the Vermont snow.

• Poking around in the garage is also a kind of research. We might spot those wild plastic snow toboggans kids use. Hey, why not? Snowboards, surfboards, skis, too. Now that's popular reference all right.

The fourth and fifth constants: Visual communication and skills

• In order to build the sled we need a craftsperson — in this case, your sister. How are we to tell her what sizes and types of material to use? How do we want her to assemble it? Better get the design down on paper. Put in three views or elevations of the front, side and top, maybe a drawing showing all three sides together. These draw-

ings give her an idea of how the finished object should look.

• Remember that other people saw how wonderfully the sled worked and wanted to buy one. So we have to make a model and a color rendering to show prospective buyers what sled will look like.

The sixth constant: Technology

• Since we are going to make more than one sled, we need to set up a way to fabricate material and assemble the parts efficiently. The easier it is to make them, the cheaper the sleds will be. Understanding technology allows you to take advantage of the materials and the construction.

The seventh constant: Evaluation

• Finally, we have to continually evaluate the product: Does it work as we planned? Are the customers satisfied? Were the materials used efficiently? Are we minimizing damage to the environment? Is blue a good color for the sides? Can we raise the price if we add racing stripes?

Does everyone apply the constants in the same way?

• It seemed rather simple when the problem was first stated. Maybe you can't see why we should apply the constants. After all, it isn't a terribly complicated device. But most design problems will be harder than this. It is important to learn how to use these constants.

• When we get tougher problems, we have to become conscious of our thinking. Slow it down. Take it step by step. The constants are not in any particular rank of importance. You can take them in any order. But you've got to touch each constant to satisfy all the criteria, answer all the questions, and present a compelling solution.

• Some people, after seeing the brief statement, like to begin sketching. They freeze each idea on paper. Others like to go to the library or talk to another designer. Some brainstorm in large groups of colleagues or friends, and bounce countless ideas around.

• It really doesn't matter what order you work in. It's this personal style of working that makes each designer, and each design, so unique. And it is this personal way of working that makes the design profession so attractive to many people.

Home is where one starts from. — *T. S. Eliot*

Let's begin at

THE BEGINNING

— the place where the problem is revealed.

Sometimes the problem is open-ended. You can practically do what you want. In other cases, the client has such specific requirements that you are pinched in and can see only a few answers.

THE CRITERIA FOR THE DESIGN

• These limits are called *criteria* and every problem has them. The finished radio must sell for less than $13.95; the shipping container must be waxed cardboard; the client wants the box to have seven sides; it should look high-tech; it must withstand unusual temperatures; it must be completely unique and not look like anything ever created since the beginning of recorded history; it is got to look fast, exotic, and so on. As you can see, it can get pretty weird.

• Guess this one. (Hint: I mentioned it earlier.) "The device must make a clean hole in hard, but brittle, material, yet stop before it encounters the soft material below. It can be sterilized."

• Answer: a power drill, called a craniotome (p. 24), used by surgeons to open the cranium (the skull) and expose the brain during an operation.

• How about that for an engineering problem? Remember it is a tool, and therefore must also be well balanced, easy to hold — a good fit in the hands of the surgeon. It was designed by a team of doctors, engineers and industrial designers. No room for imperfection here!

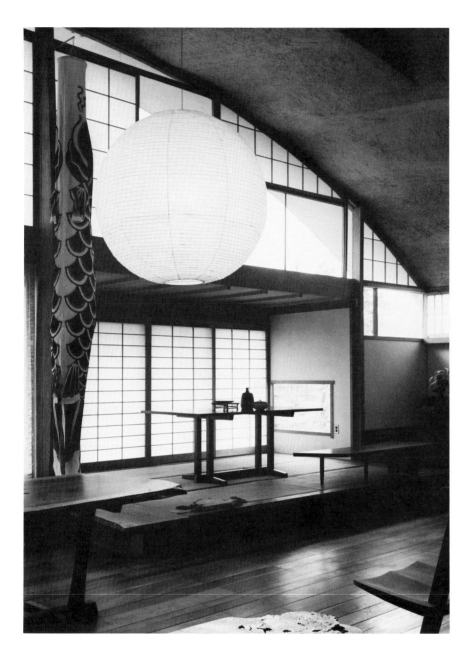

Designer George Nakashima's studio versus the Town Hall in Louvain, Belgium (opposite page). Two structures, two different purposes, same problem: How to best use enclosed space. (Nakashima photo courtesy of G. William Holland)

• Simplicity is an important quality in design. (Unless, of course, you are designing a Gothic meeting hall.) But the simpler the design, the more important each detail. When a design becomes extremely simple, it demands perfection in all details. We will see more about the power and difficulty of simplicity when we discuss logos.

A PROBLEM IN ARCHITECTURE: THE RETIREE'S PRIMARY HOME

• Let's imagine you work for a large architectural firm. Your boss calls you into the conference room to talk to a man and his wife. They have expressed an interest in having the company design a house for them. Now, a custom-designed home is a one-of-a-kind object. In most dwellings, people must make adjustments to live there comfortably. But the custom home is adjusted to the family who commissions it. You will need to interview the couple, take notes and prepare a statement that lists their demands or needs (the hard facts) and desires or dreams (the soft, variable recommendations).

• Here is where the "tire grips the road," to paraphrase an old commercial. You, the designer, have to be part good listener, part keen observer and part clever detective.

A client-driven brief

• Here is a "client-driven" design brief:

Mr. and Mrs. David Macintosh have recently purchased one acre of ocean-front property on the south shore of Long Island, New York. He is a businessman who will soon be retiring from his work in the city. Connie, his wife, was an art school graduate who would like to start weaving fine cloth. The couple has three children, two are married with two children of their own. Their other daughter, Patty, is a college student. The Macintosh's are selling their apartment in preparation for the house you have been asked to build for them.

• What else do you need to know before you start the design process? After more discussion you find out that:

✔ David wants a sailboat; it's been a life-long dream.
✔ Connie has mild arthritis.

✔ Patty will soon
  graduate and move
  to California.
✔ The couple likes to
  have the children and
  grandchildren for the
  holidays; sometimes
  they sleep over.
✔ The land is behind
  the second sand dune.
✔ This will be their
  only home.
✔ They are both good
  cooks.
✔ Neither husband nor
  wife wants to spend
  time on household
  chores and fixing-up.

• And so you write all this down too. Sometimes, you don't get to talk to the client. You're simply handed the brief itself. Another time, you might write the brief and give it to another architect to follow up.

• After collecting this information, you can begin to explore the hidden meaning underneath.

Let's play word detective

• Notice the elements that might have special meaning in this particular brief. Uncovering the impact of these elements is the task of a good designer.

The fixed criteria

• Some are strict facts, such as the location "behind the second sand dune." It is only after you know these limitations that you can find the opportunity to be creative.

The fixed criteria shape the basic focus. Everything else is up to you to interpret into a dynamic, exciting, fulfilling solution. Only the designer — the artist — has that special knowledge and insight that can raise a commonplace result to a brilliant design.

• Firstly, we must list the fixed criteria, the hard facts, those naughty bits we can't fiddle with. In this problem they are (in bold type):

> **Mr. and Mrs. David Macintosh. One acre** of **ocean front. South shore** of Long Island; he is **retiring.** The couple has **three children, two are married with two children of their own. Connie has mild arthritis. The land is behind the second sand dune. This will be their only home. Neither husband or wife want to spend their time doing household chores and fixing-up.**

The variables

• Next come the "desirables" or information that is "soft":

✔ **Connie** was an art school graduate and would like **to start weaving fine cloth.**
✔ They are **selling** their apartment **in preparation for the house.**

✔ **David** wants a **sailboat**; it's been a
life-long dream.
✔ **Patty** is a **college
student** who will soon
graduate and **move to
California.**
✔ The couple likes to have
the **children and grand-
children for the holi-
days** and **sometimes they
sleep over.**
✔ This will be their
only home.
✔ They are both **good cooks.**

• So, now you can grab a pad or a
sheet of tracing paper and a marker, and begin sketching, right?

• Wrong.
You don't know what these facts
mean yet. You have not investigat-
ed. Just the facts don't mean anything by themselves. You have to
interpret them to give them rela-
tive importance in the finished
house plan.

Refining your powers of observation:

A sleuthing skills builder
• Want to become a keen observer?
Take a tip from real detectives.
• Try this:
Go to your local mall on a crowded
evening. Let's say a Friday night.
Bring a small pad and pen. Take a

comfortable seat in an area where people hang around — on a bench near a fountain, perhaps, or at your favorite pizza parlor.

• Pick a person out of the crowd. Watch him or her closely. (Try not to be obvious or you may end up having to explain yourself.) Make a list of everything you can about the person. Height, weight, color of hair, etc. Look at the clothing and describe it.

• How does the person move: Gracefully? With quick, birdlike gestures? With a hesitant shuffle? Is the person window shopping, looking for the kids, or just waiting for a friend? Can you hear the voice? Is it gruff, smooth, accented? Continue to watch the person until you have gathered as much information as you can.

• Now have that pizza and look over your notes. Add up all the facts. Then, try to draw some conclusions from those facts to give them meaning. For example, if his glasses have a broken temple-piece, one shoelace is broken and he has a bunch of pens sticking out of his pocket, you might guess that he is a studious, absent-minded type. But if he is also wandering aimlessly, lugging a shopping bag stuffed with old clothes, he is probably one of the unfortunate homeless. To paraphrase Sherlock Holmes: *Once you eliminate everything else, whatever remains, no matter how strange, must be true.*

Distillation of your perceptions

• Another way to refine your powers of observation is through a brief writing exercise I call "distillation."

• Write a paragraph about some recent event, a personal encounter, something you saw or visited — anything with some meaning to you. After completing at least 5 or 6 sentences, look over what you wrote and choose the 15 words that mean the most to the story. Then distill those 15 words down to 7 words, and then to 4. Those four remaining words, if you chose wisely, will contain enough information to describe the basic story to someone else.

• Try it.

• You don't have to be a great writer — just a good analyzer. Once you feel that you can do this, apply the method to a design brief. After a while you'll notice that your results are sharper and more accurate.

They're talking to you — look smart!

• When talking with a client or reading a brief, don't just sit there thinking up questions or clever responses. If you do, you might miss what they are really trying to say. Concentrate on their voices. Listen carefully to every word — its inflection and spirit.

• Being a good listener makes you a much better designer. Sometimes we rely too much on our eyes. The Greek philosopher Heraclitus said, "If all things turned to smoke, the nose would be the most important organ."

Learn to listen and make your ears important receivers of information.

The 4 steps of E.B. Feldman

• A great champion of education in the arts, E.B. Feldman developed a four-stage method that we can use in designing the beach house. Feldman's four stages are:

✔ Observation
✔ Investigation
✔ Conclusion
✔ Analysis

• Each step has to be taken in proper order.

Observation

• The first step is to list the obvious without identifying the parts:

✔ Land
✔ Beach
✔ House
✔ Husband
✔ Wife
✔ Children
✔ Grandchildren
✔ Weaving, etc.

Investigation

• When we investigate these items, we can list the elements that make them unique. For instance:

✔ Beach — sand, wind, water, salt action, ocean view
✔ House — shelter, place to keep stuff, heart of family, expensive

CHAIR

There are many ways to make a chair. Designers are always searching for new methods, new materials and new structures to support the human body in a resting position. If you begin a study of the chair with a study of the body, you'll quickly see why so many pieces of furniture offend your lower half. Countless studies have told us that a seat should be around 18 inches high and 30 inches wide, and that relaxed seating should permit a back tilt of 45 to 60 degrees with a 15 degree lift under the leg. Okay then, how come so many of us are still uncomfortable?

I think some of the problem is in the materials. Plastic chairs, for example, encourage you to slide forward and tip out, and that keeps you tense — particularly at the dentist's office. Another problem is that we are all different sizes.

Unlike jeans and shoes, which eventually conform to your body, chairs resist our personal modifications. Car seating has improved. In many models you can now custom fit the seating to you. And recliners adjust, but only in angle.

Why not apply up-to-date technology to the chair? Look at examples of other products that can be customized. How about

the Reebok Pump" sneaker? Isn't the basic idea to provide a custom fit? What about shock absorbers, waterbed designs and counterweight systems like the Steadicam video and film system?

Design a chair strictly for comfort. Make it one that permits movement and shifting about, but offers support and cradling. There are some good designs around but they are concerned with style rather than comfort. You might want to find a comfortable chair; find out why it is comfortable and then improve on it.

You'll be doing a great service for all humans who have suffered and suffer still from poor seating.

- ✔ Husband — older, wants to enjoy hobby
- ✔ Wife — weaver, arthritic, grandma
- ✔ Children/Grandchildren — visit and stay for short periods

Conclusion

• In the conclusion phase we study the relationships of the parts and link them together:

• The house is the central focus for the extended family. Husband and wife want to pursue their own interests. They don't want to be burdened by home maintenance. Because they chose a beach-front location, they expect to enjoy this special environment. He might want access to a sailboat. She has arthritis, which could limit her mobility. There will be occasional visitors.

Analysis

• Finally, our analysis will tell us about our design possibilities and our design limits. Here is where we can bring together the practical and aesthetic concerns, as well as an expression of emotional content. An analysis of the beach house might look like this:

(Courtesy of Acorn Structures, Inc.)

Any home on the beach requires some basic design elements. Firstly, it must be well-insulated, particularly from the wind. The materials must be salt-resistant. They should be natural, to conform with the environment. They must also be maintenance-free. Because the land is not right on the water and an ocean view is desirable, some part of the house must have a tall elevation. At least one door must face the water for easy access to the

beach and the boat. A protected outdoor space could be used for dining, entertaining and weaving when the weather permits.

On the inside, there could be three distinct areas. One, a private space for the owners. The second, an active or living area. Lastly, an area to accommodate guests. Since the owners are older and the wife is arthritic, there is some question about building on more than one level. Stairs are difficult and can be dangerous. Since this will be the Macintosh's only home, we can assume they will live here forever. Of course, we could "step up" the guest space. A well-equipped kitchen and a large central space seem like a good expression of the owners interests.

Since the house is the focus for the extended family, it might be appropriate to have amenities (special features) like a fireplace. Lastly, in keeping with the site and the owners' preferences, there should be little formal landscaping. This keeps down the maintenance and improves the "natural" feeling.

Don't forget environmental factors. Dune erosion, shifting sands and the fragile beach eco-system are certainly a critical part of any construction on the edge of the ocean. Remember too, hurricanes sometimes batter the eastern coastline.

• At this point, a designer can sit down and develop a plan that considers the needs of his or her client.

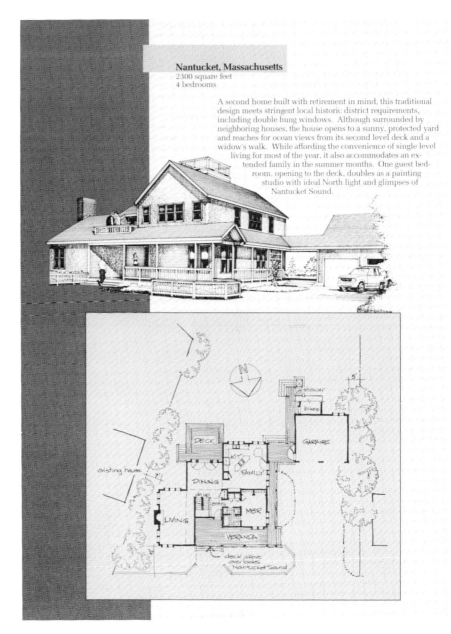

Nantucket, Massachusetts
2300 square feet
4 bedrooms

A second home built with retirement in mind, this traditional design meets stringent local historic district requirements, including double hung windows. Although surrounded by neighboring houses, the house opens to a sunny, protected yard and reaches for ocean views from its second level deck and a widow's walk. While affording the convenience of single level living for most of the year, it also accommodates an extended family in the summer months. One guest bedroom, opening to the deck, doubles as a painting studio with ideal North light and glimpses of Nantucket Sound.

The details — what exterior materials you finally choose, how you divide the space inside, what color to paint the walls — these will all be worked out with the clients.

Here's a solution for a retirement beach house in Nantucket. (Courtesy of Acorn Structures, Inc.)

A PROBLEM IN PRODUCT DESIGN: AN EMERGENCY RESPONSE

• Let's work through a design activity for a mass-produced product. Again, we'll start with the client need. Your design team is called in on an unusual but critical situation. At the first session, you hear:

A plane crash

• "Okay, I just got word that a plane full of geologists surveying Mt. McKinley has crashed. We've got at least 7 people down and alive but we can't get to them. High winds, limited visibility, and a heavy snowfall coming in 24 hours. There will be a window of clear weather in 18 hours. We've got to design and manufacture a shelter and have it ready to drop to them when the weather breaks.

• "You and you — the guy with the beard and the woman in red — you two work up a brief. Everybody else get over to engineering and inventory our materials and supplies. I'll order a small cargo plane that can fly our stuff in."

Designers to the rescue

• The guy with the beard and the woman in red — that's us. Well, we'd better outline the design activity so the team can get going on.

• First we'll identify the critical words:

A plane full of **geologists** surveying **Mt. McKinley** has crashed. We've got at least **7 people down and alive** but we **can't get to** them. **High winds, limited visibility,** and a **heavy snowfall** coming in 24 hours. There will be a window of **clear weather in 18 hours.**

Observation, investigation, conclusion, analysis.

- First, we make a list (observation):

  ✔ Geologists
  ✔ Mt. McKinley
  ✔ 7 people alive
  ✔ Can't reach them
  ✔ High winds
  ✔ Limited visibility
  ✔ Heavy snows
  ✔ Clear in 18 hours

- Then we explore the possible meaning of these items (the investigation):

  ✔ Some geologists know about wilderness survival
  ✔ Mt. McKinley is in Alaska, between Anchorage and Fairbanks.
  ✔ Seven people alive, some might be injured.
  ✔ No one can get in to give aid.
  ✔ It is constantly windy, wet and cold.

  ✔ More snow will keep them captive for more time.
  ✔ A brief amount of time to fly in and drop a shelter to them.

- The conclusion could be:

  Within 18 hours we must design and fabricate a shelter to hold seven people. Mt. McKinley is the tallest mountain in North America. Because it's windy and the geologists could be injured, the shelter must be easy to put up. It must protect the survivors from the hostile environment but be visible to rescue teams in the air. Since it will be dropped from an airplane, it must be light and compact. Only a small plane will be able to make the drop, because of the crags and peaks of the mountain.

- There are three major criteria for the shelter:

  1. Light in weight, making it easy to set up and fly in;
  2. Visible to rescuers in the air;
  3. Protection from the hostile weather (most important).

- So our analysis, given to the engineers, might read like this:

  The shelter must be light in weight. It can't have too many parts. Sections must be easy to lift and handle. They should be clearly marked for assembly. If it's too heavy it can't be dropped from a plane. If it's bulky, it won't fit through the cargo door. The shelter has to be easy to put together — no complex tools needed. It must be water-resistant and anchored in the heavy winds.
  Snow-loading is an important factor. The outside should absorb heat and have bold graphics to signal the rescue team. Condensation could form on the inside walls when they are warm. That's bad. Medical experts tell us the survivors must move about or they could get pneumonia if they are in the shelter for a long time.

- That's a pretty good analysis. Now it has to be linked to the material at hand. What's in the warehouse?

Architect Frank Gehry used cardboard to create this *Easy Edges High Chair* — so expand your mind when you think cardboard.

A little problem at the warehouse

• Uh-oh. Word just came from the warehouse. All those rolls of flame orange GoreTex we've been counting on are gone. Sold to supply the dog racers at the Itidarod. But, the warehouse still has a large store of…cardboard.

• Cardboard? Hey, don't scoff at cardboard. When treated, it can be fire-resistant and weatherproof. If bent or rolled, it can support thousands of times its own weight. It is light, easy to find and very easy to fabricate in odd-sized parts with multiple folds. You can paint on it, too.

A tower of power

• Try this great cardboard test:

• Take a strip of thin cardboard; shirt cardboard from the laundry, the back of a writing pad…Cut a strip 2" high by 12" long. Score it lightly every 2" with a used up ballpoint pen or a scissors. Then fold it back and forth into accordion folds.

• That flat piece of paper, which had no structural value, has now become a mighty tower of power.

Set the folded cardboard on edge, on a flat surface. Carefully, one at a time, place every textbook you have on top of the folded strip. If you have been careful in your folding and book placing, the strip will support more than thirty pounds of books. Weigh the cardboard against the load it supported. You'll see that the strip has supported more than a thousand times it is own weight!

the tetrahedron

the cylinder

the cube

the inflato

the umbrella

the mummy?

Meanwhile, back on the mountain

• Back to the survival problem. You can see how a clear presentation of the design activity makes for a more accurate analysis. This, in turn, leads to a more reliable design solution. The great thing about design is that there is no one right answer. There are many ways to solve a problem. All are equally good. The difference lies in how the designers emphasize what they think is the most important criteria and how that is expressed in the solution.

• An appropriate solution to the shelter problem might be flat sheets of cardboard, waxed on the outside to repel water and coated with reflective paint on the inside walls and floor to reflect body warmth. The sheets would be scored into triangles, not just to aid in folding, but to give the pattern strength. Along the edges could be velcro for secure closures. A vent would let moisture out. I'd put bright graphics on the outside surfaces so the shelter could be spotted by the rescue teams. Since the pieces are flat to begin with, they are easy to transport. They're lightweight but strong and frozen fingers won't need tools to put the shelter together.

• One problem with the cardboard shelter could be "skimming." When you drop the flat sheets from a height, they might skip along the air currents and wind up far from the drop zone.

• Oh, well, back to the drawing board.

A PROBLEM IN COMMUNICATIONS: GRAPHIC DESIGN AND POLITICS

• Here is one last example of the approach you should take in the design activity.

We're not going to take it anymore

• Your neighbors are angry about conditions in the area. Garbage collection is bad; the streets need fixing; the sidewalks are cracking. And still local taxes keep going up. The homeowners, the landlords, apartment tenants and local merchants get together and air their feelings at a town meeting. But little change occurs.

• So the group forms a political party and chooses five candidates of their own to run for office. It's a very mixed group: a local doctor, a retired schoolteacher, a bus driver, a former hippie turned banker, and you — a graphic designer. You've got to get your message out to the entire town. You want to make everyone aware — and concerned — about the problem. After all, you reason, if it can happen in our neighborhood, yours is next!

"Great neighbors make neighborhoods great!"

• You decide that you need a slogan — a war cry. The election group comes up with "Great Neighbors Make Neighborhoods Great!" This slogan will appear on posters, handbills and mailings.

R. Buckminster Fuller
(American, 1895-1983)

DYMAXION CAR

ered the universal man of modern engineering. His Dymaxion House (1929) was a six-sided machine for living. Although he was always appreciated, it's only now that we can fully understand the flexibility, low cost and brilliance of his designs.

Sometimes called the ultimate design visionary, "Bucky" Fuller created unique and wonderfully futuristic designs. Although he had little formal training, his study of mathematics and structure led to the design of the geodesic dome. By using materials placed under tension, he created a self-supporting dome that needed no interior walls or bracing.

• His experiments in alternative technology led to the Dymaxion car in 1932. Created for urban travel, the first model was a three wheeler, steered from the single back wheel. It could have been a real solution to city congestion. Fuller is consid-

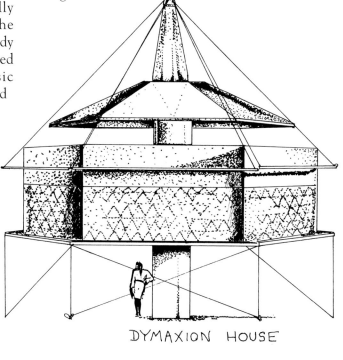

DYMAXION HOUSE

But that's not enough. You'll also need buttons, emblems and bumper stickers. Obviously, you can't always use the whole slogan. So a symbol of some kind will be necessary, too. Since you are the graphic designer, the job falls to you.

• In a perfect world, you would whip out your felt tip pen and sketch a few champion ideas. Everyone on the committee would shout: *Yes! Yes, that's it!* But in reality you'll have to explain and defend your concept. And you don't even know yet what you want it to do. That hasn't been decided. Who will get the symbol? Campaign workers, the general public, the radio and television people?

The design brief

• You had better write out a design brief. It could read like this:

> The party is determined to get its slate of candidates elected to the town council. Neighborhood support will not be enough so the **whole town**, **every neighborhood**, must be made aware of the **environmental problems.** Since a slogan has already been adopted for use, the **committee** feels

that a **symbol** of some type will add to the party's visibility among voters. It should have something to do with the environment, **garbage collection**, **bad roads and high taxes**. It must be effective on a **badge or button**; a **letterhead**, or on the **side of a bus**. It should be easily **recognizable.**

• The list of important words:

✔ whole town
✔ every neighborhood
✔ environmental problems
✔ committee
✔ symbol
✔ garbage collection, bad roads and high taxes
✔ badge or button
✔ letterhead
✔ side of a bus
✔ recognizable

• These elements mean that:

✔ The whole town is involved
✔ All neighborhoods could have the same problems or concerns
✔ The concerns are generally about the environment

✔ A committee is a group of people who share a common purpose
✔ A symbol is a method of visual communication
✔ Garbage collection, bad roads and high taxes are special issues
✔ The symbol must work in both very small and very large places

• The conclusion:

The symbol will be seen by the whole town. It will work with the slogan. There are environmental problems (garbage and bad roads) and also the problem of high taxes. A group of people, who are very different in personality but agree on this cause, will decide on the final design. It will be applied to business communications as well as billboards and buses.

• Therefore you must consider:

✔ The image. Should it be a sign (a mark that looks like what its supposed to represent) or a true symbol (which is abstract, having no representational meaning)?

✔ Letterforms or pictographs?

✔ Should it incorporate the slogan?

✔ Color. Should color be aesthetic or should it mean something?

✔ Simplicity or complexity. The symbol is going to be seen by many different types of people of different ages, ethnic backgrounds and values. And it is going to be selected by an untrained group of people

✔ It should be dynamic, vibrant and recognizable. Its meaning should be easily understood.

• At this point we have a useful analysis that will help you on the design mission. However you develop the design, you will now be clear about the purpose of the symbol, who must use it and the effects you hope it will have. From here you can make choices based on more criteria. (A button is generally round. Should your design relate to a circle?) You can also bring in aesthetic or appearance issues. Here are some samples of promising solutions:

Does the design brief stunt creativity?

• In this study, the role of the design brief has been to take random, chaotic ideas and elements and assemble them in a meaningful way to help clarify your thinking. Some people, especially student designers, see this step by step sequence as interfering with their energy and drive.

• Well, that's true to some extent. And for a very few really, really gifted individuals, this process might be unnecessary. But for everyone else, even after you hit the jackpot a few lucky times, your good guessing, your intuition, will still be unreliable. You'll need the support of a method that brings in consistent results.

• You see, applying a model like this one will grant you freedom in the later stage of the process — in fact, in the one coming up right now. It's in the analysis stage that ideas come alive. It's where you can throw off the ropes that hold you back and spew out great heaps of genius. Of course, the more ideas you have, the more ideas you get, and then the more ideas you use, which can result in more choices, which means that you can choose from a larger number of possible winners, therefore…. You get my drift?

Nature's architecture — Form created by function. (Radiograph courtesy of Eastman Kodak Co.)

Where do

GREAT

ideas

come

from?

How can we get ideas to solve problems creatively?

A bicycle shed is a building. Lincoln Cathedral is a piece of Architecture.
— Sir Nikolaus Pevsner (1961)

FINDING INSPIRATION

• To create you must first design. This means that you need a consistent approach to get to an answer.

Nature as designer

• How would nature have designed it? Some designers feel that answering this question is the way to a quality solution. Sometimes, it is a good measuring stick. But I'm not quite sure how nature would have designed a video tape recorder or a blender.

The organic designs of Luigi Colani

• For an example of a designer inspired by natural (organic) form, take a look at the work of Luigi Colani. His designs of everything, from cameras to kitchens, have the appearance and feel of growing, living things.

The inturning spiral

• Some shapes and forms are common to humanity. This means they always strike everybody the same way because of their logic or their universal correctness. Did you know, for example, that when people are lost they tend to travel in an inward circle, a spiral? If you blindfold a swimmer or a driver of an automobile, they are inevitably drawn in circles toward a center point. Back in 1928, a professor of zoology at the University of Kansas, Asa A. Schaeffer, tested this theory. He found that instinct takes control of a person when the other senses are of little use. And that when they acted instinctively, they made these inturning spirals.
• What does this mean for a designer?

The golden mean

• The Greek mathematician, Pythagoras, who was a keen observer of nature, noticed that many, totally different species and lifeforms appeared to have a simi-lar basic design. For instance, the petals of a daisy unfold in a pattern that looks like the shell of some snails. He found he could express this pattern in mathematical terms and then model it into accurate, harmonic, musical scales.
• This design is known as the golden mean, or golden rectangle.
• When you look closely at the freedom and randomness of nature, you come to realize there really is a type of order common to every living thing. The golden mean is a geometric expression of that ideal. It can be described as rectangles within rectangles, that get smaller and smaller yet are always in the same proportion.
• People often show an unconscious pref-erence for the golden mean. It can be seen in the sizes of paper money, checks and even credit cards. Most of us find the proportions of those shapes comfortable. It comes from a natural desire to make order out of chaos or randomness.

Should every design be golden?

• Does all this talk about nature and organic forms mean that every design problem has a mathematical solution? Can we just follow scientific or natural models and create useful objects that everyone finds beautiful to hold and behold? Personal taste is an important part of our designed environment. Some people might like everything in perfect proportion. Then again, natural design can turn off as many people as it turns on. Modern humans want to be challenged, excited, even upset by unique, unnatural shapes, textures, images and forms.

Creativity takes chances

• Our ability to design for ourselves, from raw materials, not just out of necessity but for pleasure, is one thing that separates us from other species. We should take advantage of this difference. If we are to rise to the mission of creating design, we have to take risks. We have to go far from the comfortable shores of safe and reliable solutions toward dangerous unchartered waters.

In this early development sketch for Canon camera, Luigi Colani shows his interest in natural or "bio-form." Why would a Japanese camera company be interested in his style? (Hint - go back to the Japanese Shrine picture on page 12.)

• When fog prevents a sailor from sighting a buoy, he turns his boat in tight circles until he makes enough waves to rock the buoy and make it clang. By causing a disturbance in the water, he finds where his course lies. In design, you've got to be willing to make a few waves — to take risks in order to succeed. As the poet Robert Frost said, "What's worth succeeding in, is worth failing in." Sailors who stay in the harbor never get into danger. But then, they never get anywhere either.

• Most of us, when faced with a job to do, don't really think about it. How many times have we been asked to solve a problem of some kind, whether writing an essay or building a box kite, and we immediately fix on some way, usually the first way, to finish the task. We just want to make the job go away. So we just plod along in a linear, or direct way to the solution.

• For every answer you achieved, you ignored zillions of other possible, just-as-right or even better answers. You might say: yes, but I did get the right answer. But is there really only one right answer? And did you find the best one? The one that would excite you the most? That's what makes great designers — the ability to throw out what a lesser designer might think is good.

• There is not just one right way

Nautilus shell.

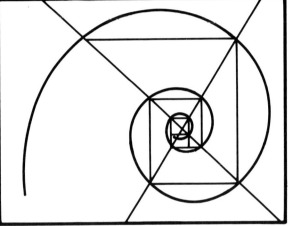

Look at the relationship of the nautilus and the golden rectangle. You might compile a file of those natural objects whose forms have been used as mechanical references.

to do things. There are always other ways. That's where we are going now — to the galaxy of many answers. We are going to explore how to get them, generate them, make them up. For the more answers you develop, the easier it will be to get the very best.

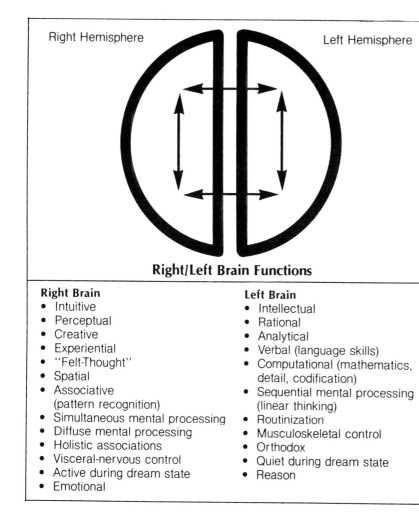

Right/Left Brain Functions

Right Brain
- Intuitive
- Perceptual
- Creative
- Experiential
- "Felt-Thought"
- Spatial
- Associative (pattern recognition)
- Simultaneous mental processing
- Diffuse mental processing
- Holistic associations
- Visceral-nervous control
- Active during dream state
- Emotional

Left Brain
- Intellectual
- Rational
- Analytical
- Verbal (language skills)
- Computational (mathematics, detail, codification)
- Sequential mental processing (linear thinking)
- Routinization
- Musculoskeletal control
- Orthodox
- Quiet during dream state
- Reason

STRATEGIES FOR CREATIVITY

- There are two very different stages in getting ideas: idea generation, where you get as many ideas as possible; and idea selection, where you choose the best answer to a given problem. Many of the techniques from here on are intended to generate a volume of ideas. Evaluating these ideas and choosing the right solution will come later.

The big B

- Most of these techniques for generating ideas fall under the big umbrella title called brainstorming. Basically brainstorming is a way to get every possible aspect of a problem and solution out of your head and into sight.

How to brainstorm

- When you brainstorm, there should be an unrestrained, unedited, uncriticized offering of ideas by all members of a group or team looking for solutions. One person can do it alone by yelling aloud to the walls, or better still, writing down every last idea that pops into one's head. But brainstorming works best as a group activity.
- Brainstorming can reveal new choices and make you aware of the different ways you can get to a solution. It helps to generate alternative ways of seeing and answering a problem. The rules are very simple:

- ✔ All ideas are acceptable.
- ✔ There is no editing, modifying or commenting on anyone else's ideas.
- ✔ There must be an atmosphere of freedom and play. This allows people to say anything even remotely connected to the problem.

A brainstorming session

• One way to get started is to write the design activity on a chalkboard or giant sheets of paper. Sit down in a circle, read the brief aloud and just go from there. Ask provocative questions:

- ✔ What is its purpose?
- ✔ How will it work?
- ✔ Who uses it?
- ✔ What should it feel like?

It doesn't all have to sound like a questionnaire. You can get outrageous:

- ✔ If you were the object, how would you taste, feel, smell?
- ✔ Would you be warm or cool?
- ✔ Describe the object without mentioning its name (kind of like charades) (I can do this; I feel like this; people like me because I am...)

You can try role-playing:

- ✔ I am the client and I want...
- ✔ I am the object and I am...

• Tease your fellow designers with "what if" questions. Pass large sheets of paper around the room and write down everything! In this "ideation" stage, the more ideas the better. Having many ideas improves your chances of having one great one. Remember, nothing is more dangerous than an idea, when it is the only one you have.

• If you are having difficulty getting a good sized list, bring out the following weapons:

• Some special techniques (via Alex Osborne):

SCAMPER:

Substitute:
- ✔ What could you substitute?
- ✔ What might be done instead?
- ✔ What could be done different or better?

Combine:
- ✔ What could you combine?
- ✔ What would work well together?
- ✔ What could be forced together?

Adapt:
- ✔ What could be adjusted to suit a purpose or condition?
- ✔ How could something be made to fit?

Magnify, Minimize, Modify:
- ✔ What if you changed the form or quality?
- ✔ Could it be made larger, greater, stronger?
- ✔ Could it be smaller, lighter, slower?

Put to other uses:
- ✔ How could you use it for a different purpose?
- ✔ What are new ways to apply it?

Eliminate:
- ✔ What could you subtract or take away?
- ✔ What could you do without?

Reverse:
- ✔ What would you have left if it were reversed, or turned around?
- ✔ Could you change the parts, orders, order, layout or sequence?

Forced connections

• Another type of creative thinking is called forced connections. If you list all the criteria of a project or problem and divide the items into categories, some interesting connections can show up.

• In a house problem, for example, you could make lists for the exterior, the interior space, the family, the site and the specific requirements. Under each heading, list your ideas (such as cedar siding under exterior). When you have a large enough list, start to connect elements in one category with elements in another. Watch what happens. It can lead to a different way of thinking about the solution.

Synectics and innovative thinking

- There are two other methods that can generate ideas: synectics and innovative thinking.

- Quite a bit of this information comes from two noted experts, Nicholas Roukes and Roger von Oech. In spite of their different backgrounds — Roukes is a design professor, and von Oech is a consultant to industry — their ideas will definitely prove useful to anyone studying design and design communication.

- There is some repetition in the two approaches. But the two techniques are applied in very different ways. So don't worry if you see the same term or idea more than once.

- Of course, other models exist, too. I heard comedian Rita Rudner say, "I don't worry if I get lost. I just change my destination." Worth pondering sometimes, I think.

Synectics

- Synectics comes from the Greek "synectikos," which means "holding together." In synectics, apparently unrelated objects are put together to create a different way of seeing a problem or situation.

- When you press hard for a logical solution and nothing seems to be happening, it is sometimes better to bypass the logical part of your brain and use native intelligence. This is the mind power hidden in your emotional and psychological make-up. Although it is an instinctive talent, most people have to learn (or relearn) native

ANALOGY

IMAGING

WOULDN'T IT BE A STRANGE WORLD IF....

...SCHOOL WAS A BIG SENSE-SURROUND.

...CARTOONS CREATED HUMANS.

intelligence because schools teach you to ignore it in favor of logic.

Synectic strategies

- To think "synectically," you need an attitude of creative play. Here are six synectic strategies to help you do this.

1. Analogy: The similarity between things can be used to make comparisons. For instance, you could compare the skeleton of a man to the trunk and branches of a tree, or the human nervous system to electrical wiring. You could also play the role of an electron and imagine the trip you might take. What would the world be like from the point of view of an ant?

- Contradictory figures of speech

SIGNS, SYMBOLS

PEAS BE WITH YOU   PRISONER OF BELIEFS

MULTIPLE PERSON

SPONTANEOUS COMBUST   LOW TUNNEL

DREAM SYMBOLISM

Upper right: hobo symbols (Reproduced with permission from Henry Dreyfuss and Associates, 1991)

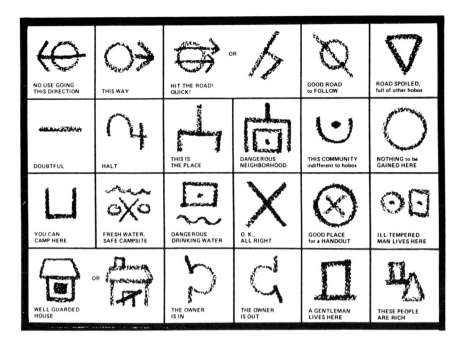

NO USE GOING THIS DIRECTION	THIS WAY	HIT THE ROAD! QUICK! or		GOOD ROAD to FOLLOW	ROAD SPOILED, full of other hobos
DOUBTFUL	HALT	THIS IS THE PLACE	DANGEROUS NEIGHBORHOOD	THIS COMMUNITY indifferent to hobos	NOTHING to be GAINED HERE
YOU CAN CAMP HERE	FRESH WATER, SAFE CAMPSITE	DANGEROUS DRINKING WATER	O.K., ALL RIGHT	GOOD PLACE for a HANDOUT	ILL-TEMPERED MAN LIVES HERE
WELL-GUARDED HOUSE or		THE OWNER IS IN	THE OWNER IS OUT	A GENTLEMAN LIVES HERE	THESE PEOPLE ARE RICH

are a type of analogy, making unexpected connections: "the living dead," "quiet noise," "wonderfully evil." Using analogy to develop solutions for design problems is a natural way to continue the brainstorming process.

2. Imaging: Mental images are a powerful source of ideas. Everybody has images, dreams and daydreams. Bring them out and use them. You can practice this by imagining colors while listening to music, feeling textures while you smell a fragrance.

• The brain is divided into two halves: the right controls intuition, creativity, emotion; the left controls logic, reason, verbal and mathematic functions. To heighten your creativity, you've got to play on the right side of the brain by strengthening your powers of observation, memory and fantasy.

3. Signals, Signs and Symbols: Signals, according to Roukes, are messages perceived by the senses by means of light, temperature, color, smell, sound, etc. Signs are signals that we interpret as having special meaning. (The sound of thunder is a sign of approaching storm.)

• Symbols express meaning indirectly. Artists use symbols to communicate fear, moods and sensations. Doodles, the alphabet, abstract art — these are all symbols standing for other things.

4. Myths: Like dreams, myths take place in a special time and space. Whether they are told to entertain (storytelling), as part of a ritual (religious tales), or to describe the origin or beginning of something,

The Tower of Babel — a symbol of a breakdown in communication. (Courtesy of Kunsthistorisches Museum, Vienna)

myths generally have the ability to say "the moral of the story is…"

• Every myth contains a disguised message. Heroes and villains, television personalities, and science fiction are all part of our modern myths. When you start to solve a design problem, you can use story or legend as a place to begin. If two old radios were talking together in a second-hand store, what would they have to say about their great-grandchildren?

5. Rituals, Games and Performance: We learn at an early age to behave in a "civilized" manner. Some rules for conduct are casual, like at a party; some are formal, like at a funeral. Games challenge skills and luck, physically and mentally,

cooperatively or competitively. Rituals are a special kind of game with very special rules. Performance gives the artist a chance to express ideas as concepts in action.

• Creating a ritual mask with a magical function (making Sally's boyfriend into a toad), creating a miniature environment to contain one person, inventing a game based on an alien civilization — these are all projects that heighten your awareness of the rules. They can show how to work within and around the rules. A great skill for a designer!

Ritual masks serve many purposes — to make the supernatural become visible, depict fabled ancestors, or represent powerful spirits. (Songye Mask, Zaire, Africa. Courtesy of University of Pennsylvania Museum)

RITUAL GAMES, PERFORMANCE

THE CIRCLE OF 'SOUL' DISPLAY

THE RITUAL OF THE 'HEAD TIP' AND THE 'LAYING OF HOT DOGS.'

PARADOX

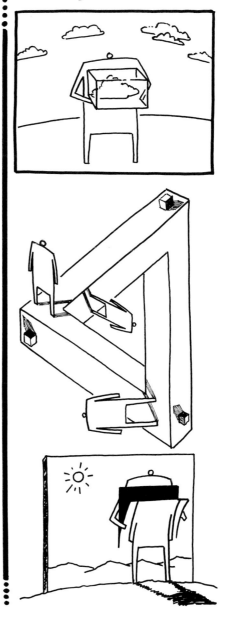

6. Paradox: An image, statement or situation that defies logic. Take three pictures from a magazine: say, a beach scene, a sewing machine, a mound of trash. If you combine these into one image, you would no longer have three separate ideas but rather one image with a new meaning. A paradox cannot be explained. It remains a mystery that each of us interprets a bit differently.

• List fifty objects and randomly chose two. If you create an art object representing the marriage of these two, you will be creating a paradox.

• Use these six strategies as a warm-up to design, as a game to heighten creativity once a group has started on a solution, or even when you get stuck in an uncomfortable place during the design process. This type of thinking can act as a liberating force.

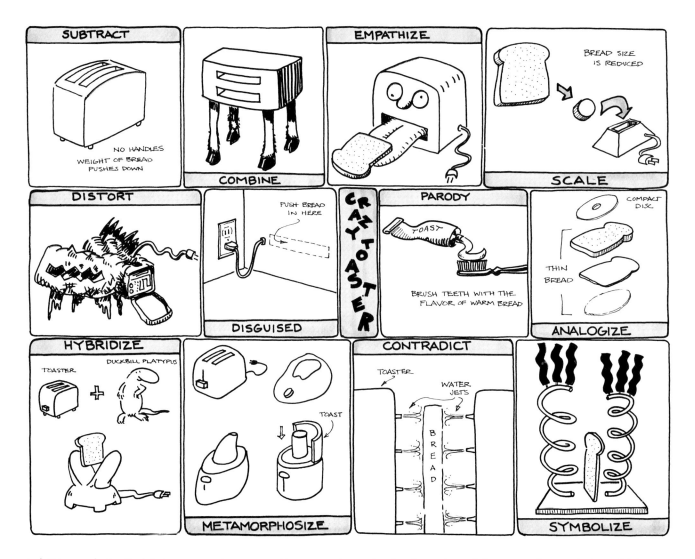

Apply "trigger mechanisms" to designing a toaster and you come up with some unusual approaches. How about working with this creative technique in the design of clothes, cars, musical instruments or space vehicles?

*Hybridize. (Johnny Hart, **B.C.**, 1986. Courtesy of the artist and Creators Syndicate, Los Angeles)*

Triggers for synectic thinking

• Roukes also identifies "trigger mechanisms." These are specific ways to crank up your mental motor.

1. **Subtract:** Simplify, eliminate, dispose of the unnecessary, abbreviate.
2. **Repeat:** Echo, restate, duplicate, control the sequence of events.
3. **Combine:** Mix, arrange, merge; combine materials, connect dissimilar things.
4. **Add:** Expand, magnify, advance in time.
5. **Transfer:** Move the subject into a new situation or out of its natural environment, change the setting in time or history.
6. **Empathize:** Give your subject human qualities. Become the object. Relate to it emotionally.
7. **Superimpose:** Overlap ideas on top of one another to create something new.
8. **Change scale:** Make the miniature gigantic and the huge microscopic. Change the proportions.
9. **Fragment:** Split it into bits and examine them separately.
10. **Isolate:** Choose one element, crop it like a picture and examine it in detail.
11. **Distort:** Bend it out of shape. Make it fatter, weirder, melt it, crush it. Rip it apart and put it back together in a different way.
12. **Disguise:** Camouflage it, deceive the viewer. Create a meaning for the subconscious.
13: **Contradict:** Take the original purpose and flip it. Contradict gravity, time, human anatomy. Doublethink it: give it two meanings and accept both as important.
14. **Parody:** Make it bizarre. Make it a caricature. Transform it into a visual pun or joke.
15. **Prevaricate:** Bend the truth, fictionalize, fantasize. Purposefully mislead or confuse.
16. **Analogize:** Compare, seek similarities, make metaphors.
17. **Hybridize:** Marry your subject to an unlikely mate. Combine color, materials, organic and inorganic elements.
18. **Metamorphose:** Imagine your subject changing. Picture the changes in sequence or entirely out of order.
19. **Symbolize:** Give your object a visual reference by making it into a symbol of something else.
20. **Mythologize:** Build a myth or story around your subject. Transform the object into a mythological idol.
21. **Fantasize:** Trigger preposterous ideas, "what-if" thoughts like "if cars were made of clay…," "if bees were six feet long…," "if cats were the dominant species on earth…"

Step outside yourself

- This is a pretty big list. It contains acts of construction and destruction; change, reflection, fun and mild insanity. To invent, to create, you've got to be ready to destroy and break down as well. This attitude — a willingness to explore outwardly and examine inwardly — permits you to profit from these techniques.

- If you'd like to succeed and be creative while others merely answer and survive, you've got to step outside your normal self and be someone else. Albert Szent-Gyorgyi said: "Discovery consists of looking at the same thing as everyone else and thinking something different."

Innovative thinking

- Roger von Oech, in his book, *A Whack on the Side of the Head*, is convinced we have the keys to open mental locks that keep us from being creative. Sometimes, he says, you've got to knock down or "whack" the accepted ways of doing things through special techniques. Here are the mental locks that are holding us back:

1. "The right answer"

- In education especially, teachers helped us get the right answer. But along the way we lost the ability to be imaginative. You've got to learn to look at the second and third and fourth answers as being just as correct. Ask different questions. Not "what should this hammer look like?" But rather "how does the hand work?"

2. "That's not logical"

- The two sides of the brain, right and left, think differently. Von Oech calls these soft and hard thinking. Hard is logical, precise, and adult; soft is metaphoric, playful and childlike. A hard thinker would ask what materials these chairs should be made of; a soft thinker might ask what the chairs might look like if our knees bent the other way.

- The metaphor is a powerful force for creative inspiration. It helps us understand one idea by using another. For example:

  ✔ Life is an elevator. It has lots of ups and downs and someone is always pushing your buttons.
  ✔ Life is a maze in which you try to avoid the exit.

Use the metaphor as a tool to expand your thinking about a problem.

3. "Follow the rules"

- Don't color outside the lines. Raise your hand to answer a question. We encourage rule following. It helps keep order, but doesn't encourage new thinking. Sometimes you have to break out of one pattern to discover another.

- Walk to school a different way, change your style of clothing. Look at patterns and imagine what could happen if they are changed. Tendencies of behavior (*if I smile at the fast food counter girl, she'll*

smile back); processes (*convert flour, eggs and milk into waffles*); cultural rites (*dating, going steady, marriage*) are all patterns. If we break the rules, we can make new patterns.

4. *"Be practical"*
• Forget it!
• Ask "what-if" questions. What if we had seven fingers on each hand? How would this affect sports, computer keyboards, the number system? What if people lived to be 200 years old? What products would they need? What would

happen if we made a product uglier or out of some weird material?
• Every person is both an artist and a judge. Don't let the practical judge evaluate until after you create, or nothing will happen.

5. *"Avoid ambiguity"*
• Sometimes it is in our best interest as creators to be vague rather than precise. If you were asked to draw a picture of yourself in a position of movement and provide a device to support that position, what would you be mak-

ing? Furniture, of course, but unusual and interesting furniture. If I simply told you to create a bed or chair, your designs would probably be traditional and regular.

• Before you design, listen to comedy recordings or read comic books. Humor plays tricks on logic and that's what ambiguity is all about. Write an ambiguous description of a design brief and see if your teammates can guess what the object is.

6. *"To err is wrong"*

• It's amazing that ball players can make millions of dollars a year for consistent failure. A .300 hitter fails to reach base seven out of ten times at bat. And he's a hero.

• If you want the hits, be prepared for the misses. If you are afraid to be wrong, you aren't going to take many chances. Those who stick their heads up, sometimes get them shot off. Risk-takers are apt to fail but when they succeed, they succeed big.

7. *"Play is frivolous"*

• When do you get good ideas? Some people say, when they're faced with a deadline or when things break down. But just as many people say they get good ideas when they're fooling around, toying with a problem or doing something entirely unrelated. Great ideas can come during physical exercise, when the mind is free to roam.

• Play, and its child, fun, are not

only good — they're necessary. Make your work space a fun place to be. Surround yourself with things that make you feel good.

8. *"That's not my area"*

• Everything in the world can be a source for great ideas. Don't ignore the unusual. Travel, plan special activities or get into different situations that can "whack" you. Look in junk yards, in magazines for specialty interests or professions (sanitation collection, medicine, millionaires); flea markets, magic acts, cheap how-to books. You might find solutions to your problem in a completely unrelated field.

9. *"Don't be foolish:"*

• Wrong.

• Get rid of your "stupid" monitor and act accordingly. What would happen if you faced the rear on an elevator? If you wore your underwear on the outside? If you walked down the halls of your school "squaring the corners?" The group can't stand people who don't conform. Practice foolish behavior and avoid "groupthink."

10. *"I'm not creative"*

• You are if you think you are.

• Like anything else, when you meet with a bit of creative success, you will want more. If you succeed in solving a problem in a clever way then, lo and behold, you'll know you're creative. All your future work will be approached

DESIGN
Challenge

EATING TOOL

The first table forks appeared in Italy in the eighth century. They fell out of use, then returned for good in the fourteenth century. They had two tines (prongs) and were used in royal homes, replacing the knife as the food-holding tool. Eventually, by 1850, the fork grew two more tines, with a curved shape.

In North America, colonists were slow to give up their two-knife system, going first to a knife and spoon (one to cut and the other to bring the food to the mouth). Since the fork was the hardest instrument to manufacture it took quite a bit longer to gain popular use.

Our current eating habits call for all three implements. Sometimes, when camping for instance, the tools are in a set that fits together. The famous Swiss Army Knife often includes both fork and spoon within a collapsible instrument.

I wonder if our use of all three tools is becoming outdated. Processed foodstuffs, food from other cultures, microwave technology and fast food all suggest that new, additional or replace-ment implements might be useful. An interesting question arises: did foods and ways of preparing foods create the need for certain types of tools? Or did the development of table tools influence the way each culture prepared their foodstuffs? Your assignment: create a tool that will be universal. One that can cut, hold, spear and convey food from plate to mouth. It could be one handle with multi-function heads, multiple handles, rotational parts, or any number of possibilities. Or it could have just one simple part that can do everything.

Keep in mind the nature of the job to be done, the types of food people eat now, the ergonomic considerations (your hand and mouth) and even the idea of left- or right-handedness.

Courtesy of Bissel and Wilhite Co.

The Linn Cove viaduct, part of the Blue Ridge Parkway in North Carolina, was an innovation in construction. By designing the roadway in segments, engineers solved two problems — building the highway and minimizing environmental destruction. (Courtesy of Figg & Muller Engineers, Inc.)

with that mindset. Believe in the value of your ideas. Play, be willing to look foolish, and seek opportunities to be whacked.

A toaster is a toaster is a toaster

• Keep in mind that a product, a building or a graphic design isn't always what you think it is. A toaster, for example, does not make toast. It is an electric device that controls the burning of bread. And if bread wasn't a thin square of flour, water and yeast, 4x4x3/4", if it was an analog or imitation, or a compressed material the size of an aspirin, then a toaster is no longer a toaster — is it?

• Another example: What is architecture? What is the nature of architecture? These sound like the same question, but they have completely different answers.

• Architecture can be defined as the art or science of enclosing space, creating shelter, a gathering place for work, for living, etc. The nature of architecture, however, is something quite different. Architecture is primarily a destructive act. When we build, we destroy the natural environment, add to the problem of waste disposal, steal precious water from the earth, squeeze more people into smaller spaces and affect environments far, far away. Architects who recognize the destructive nature of architecture seek to minimize the impact of building on the global environment.

• When you look at a problem from a different angle, different answers emerge. Choosing the better answer is a balancing act among many possibilities. Often, design is a compromise, taking the best from many sources to make the most effective answer.

• Sometimes we get so attached to an idea, compromise is unthinkable. It was said earlier, and it's worth repeating: the more ideas generated, the more chances that the eventual solution will be powerful and successful.

• Having come this far in our design travels, your powers of analysis can now be tested. Go back to the three design briefs: the Macintosh house, the survival shelter and the political logo. Apply the strategies we've looked at in this chapter. I have no doubt that the amount of ideas and the quality of your possible answers have already expanded far beyond your first attempts.

Le Corbusier

(Charles-Edouard Jeannert, Swiss–French, 1887–1965)

Architectural bio-form: Le Corbusier's Notre-Dame-du-Haut Chapel, Ronchamp, France.

An architect, painter, furniture designer and theorist, Le Corbusier had tremendous influence on design in this century. After working in architectural offices, he settled in Paris in 1917 and by 1925 exhibited furniture designs and other mass-produced items. He used tubular steel with leather and other natural fabrics to achieve a modern and luxurious effect.

His architecture at first concentrated on mass-produced housing and town planning. Later it became very personal and easily identifiable. Most of the structures were supported, raised off the ground on columns, and appeared sculptural and expressive. He is often contrasted with Walter Gropius for they had similar training, used the same materials (concrete, glass and steel), yet achieved completely different effects.

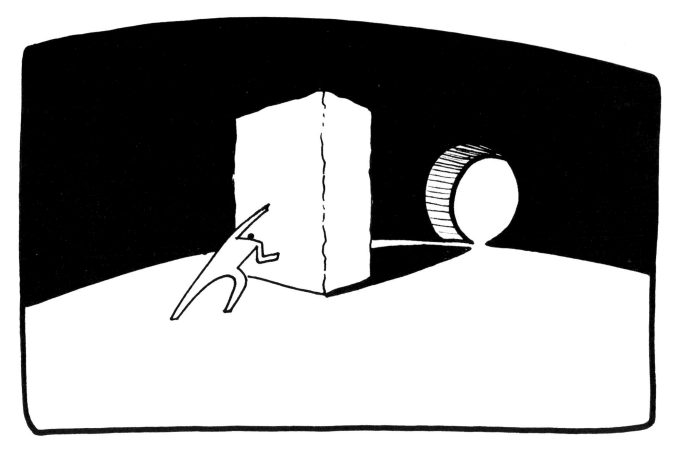

For every problem, there is one solution that is neat, simple and wrong. — H. L. Mencken

How does the
mind connect

MANY DIFFERENT FACTS

AND REARRANGE

them into new

patterns

We're not sure how so-lutions occur to those who seek answers. We do know however that design is a social act. Each one of us is the sum of our social experiences plus our formal training, such as school. We are people first and design students second. Therefore, our ability to solve design problems depends on our personal history as well as our professional training.

• Who we are, what we've seen, where we've been, what we've learned and how we think of ourselves — these all affect our designs.

THE VOCABULARY OF DESIGN

• People have been making things to use since history began. Everything designed today has a source way back. The values of an age — the moral climate, politics, economics — all affect design. Studying the history of design allows you to build a vocabulary of previous answers. Like a vocabulary of words, this vocabulary of design can put together in many different ways to give new and different meanings. And the larger it is, the more ways you can use it.

In this old TV we find technology that is safely hidden by furniture. (Courtesy of the Library of Congress)

Play it again, Sam

• Some philosophers think that there is nothing new to be created; it has all been done before. Others feel that technology is changing so fast that soon everything will be new all the time. But human beings hunger for a sense of time and place. When you hear a particular song on the radio, it takes you back to the moment when you first heard that song. A unique moment can be instantly recalled. You remember just what you were doing: the mood, the weather, especially who you were with.

• Whenever I smell chocolate being heated on a stove, I can see my grandmother working in her kitchen, baking on a hot afternoon. I see myself as a young boy seated at the dining room table, ready to eat her special "pinwheel" cookies.

Feeling comfortable with design

• Good designers understand the emotional need we have to be comfortable with the objects in our environment. When television came into our living rooms in the early fifties, designers tried to ease this new communication machine into the family by hiding the technology. Eight-inch televisions were encased in fancy furniture with classic doors, moldings and finishes to fit into the surroundings. On top, Mom would keep fresh flowers in a vase, surrounded by pictures of the family.

• Today, our televisions have red and green blinking lights. They shimmer with glassy black finishes. They are hard, sleek, thin and scream hi-tech across the room. We are not only comfortable with hi-tech now; we are proud of it.

Seeing the connections

• We would be foolish if we did not look back at what's been done before. In seeking new designs, we need to see the connections that existed between different design forms. Why did American car makers spawn tail fins on cars in the late fifties? What do a train locomotive, the Chrysler building and a Waring blender have in common. What connection is there between a 1935 Hamilton watch, the painting *Victory Boogie Woogie* by Piet Mondrian and a Checker Taxicab? Why are fountain pens popular again and why does the standard business uniform for men still consist of a suit and tie? How did artist Jackson Pollock help make the Swatch watch popular even though Pollock died twenty years before the first Swatch was made?

A modern version of the classic Waring Blender. (Courtesy of Waring)

William Van Alen's Chrysler Building, 1928-30, in New York City (Courtesy of Bettmann Archives). Top right: Piet Mondrian's Victory Boogie Woogie, 1944, (Courtesy of Burton Tremaine). The Checker Cab (Courtesy of Detroit Public Library). Jackson Pollack's Full fathom Five, 1947, oil on canvas, 50 7/8 x 30 1/8'' (Courtesy of The Museum of Modern Art, Gift of Peggy Guggenheim).

- Designers are people who know something about history, about current trends and popular culture (which they often help to create) and have the ability to see into the future. From rap music to street lamps to fashion footwear, designers look at everything in the culture. They look backwards, forwards and sideways all the time. To succeed in design, you'll have to do the same.

- For each problem you encounter, there is some reference material that can help you, sometimes written, sometimes visual, sometimes in a completely different form. Whether formalized in books, or from popular, "non-expert" sources, these are important elements that can make your design solutions more meaningful to a larger audience of users. Think of reference as a building supporting the top floor — your design.

Old toaster. (Courtesy of General Electric)

FORMAL REFERENCE

- Knowing where to look isn't enough. You have to know what to look for.

From toast to eternity

- Using the example of the toaster, let's map out a plan to collect as much information as possible about this common device. For a general overview, you could start with books about kitchen appliances.

- You'd learn that starting around 1900, when electricity became relatively common, bread was toasted in a gadget that bears little resemblance to the toaster we know. Big and clumsy, it usually incinerated the bread. Sometimes it set fire to whatever it stood next to. Continuing your research, you would find the first pop-up

New toaster. It still does the same thing but has been reinterpreted for a new era in design. Can you picture the early model in the kitchen pictured on page 8? (Courtesy of Black & Decker)

toaster in 1919. It included a thermostat that eliminated the burnt toast problem.

- Although materials and technological advances made it more efficient over time, the biggest changes in the toaster have been in its appearance. It was first a large and heavy thing. As technology improved and engineering limitations disappeared, the designer became free to interpret the toaster as a kind of kitchen sculpture.

Charles Sheeler's painting City Interior glorifies the structure of the industrial landscape. 1936, oil on fiber board, 22 1/8 x 27''. (Courtesy of the Worcester Art Museum)

If we stood it on end, I suppose this 1959 Cadillac Eldorado Seville would zoom skyward like a rocket. (Courtesy of GM)

The thirties toaster

- In the thirties, the "machine age," the toaster became streamlined. It featured plenty of chrome and bakelite for a sophisticated "moderne" look. It was slick, powerful, reserved.
- If you look at other reference material from the thirties, such as books, magazines and journals, you can see a similarity among architectural designs, product designs, advertising, even fashions. The Chrysler Building by William Van Alen, the S–1 locomotive by Raymond Loewy, the paintings of Charles Sheeler, the design of new typefaces — all had a similar feeling, a "thirties" feeling.

The fifties toaster

- During the 1950s, the International Style of architecture, led by Mies Van de Rohe, designed skyscrapers with clean lines, flat surfaces and geometric forms with little or no detail. At the same time, men's business suits were trim fitting with narrow lapels, thin ties and narrow legs. Smooth, slick, pared down and cool. You see the relationship?
- The fifties was also the "rocket age." Look at the tail fins on a 1959 Cadillac. The car looks like its ready to blast off. Our toaster was affected, too. Although its shape remained boxy, the surface design and trim featured vertical and diagonal patterns that reflected the times.

I. M. Pei designed the East Building of the National Gallery of Art, Washington, D.C. A tree grows up from the floor and an Alexander Calder mobile hangs from the space-frame skylight roof. (Courtesy of the National Gallery of Art)

The nineties toaster

• Today is the age of "hi-tech." A kitchen may still be the "heartbeat" of the house, but it is now the "engineering center," too. We love to show off the controls on our appliances. They showcase the microprocessor and computer brains that we have created to deal with our necessities.

• Firms like Frogdesign and Lunar Design and architects like I. M. Pei like to highlight technology. They make users aware of the engineering inside of the object. Others, such as M & Co., Tom Bonauro and Robert A. M. Stern, try to soften the impact of technology — the way the first televisions were softened. They put a friendlier face on their designs, making the objects look like an older style modernized.

The historical context of design

• The point is that formal research, whether from an encyclopedia, from design texts, trade periodicals or journals, helps you uncover the relationships that exist between the object, the user of the object, the times in which the object exists and you, the designer. To really understand a design, you must know the influences acting on all of society at the time the object was developed.

• Even if you want to break away from the traditional and do something radical, go against the trend, you should understand the historical context. Then you can use it, or ignore it on purpose. This knowledge can be gained only by research.

• When asked to design a toaster, you've got to know kitchen history and architectural history. But you should also research what people were doing in the thirties, fifties, or whenever. Understand their clothing, music, slang, sports. What influenced what? Sometimes it is hard to tell.

• Different cultures, different races, people who live in different parts of the country, sometimes people of different religion or economic status — all have their own unique perspective on designed objects. Good designers "know the territory." They understand their audience and relate object to user.

- You've also got to research the technology of the object. What makes a toaster toast? Well, you need power, some way to transfer electrical energy into heat energy, a way to adjust the amount of heat and control the "burning." You need a place to put in bread and get out toast. These mechanisms have changed a great deal during the history of the toaster.

Reference Books

- It would be impossible to list even the more important reference volumes with which a student designer should be familiar. There is a vast number of architecture books, containing a wealth of information for the student designer: from *On Architecture* by Vitruvius (pre-Christian Rome), to Palladio's *The Four Books of Architecture* (1570), to Frank Lloyd Wright's *The Natural House* (1954).
- Industrial and product design is a younger field, so there are fewer references to study. But the giants who shaped the field — Raymond Loewy, Norman Bel Geddes, Walter Dorwin Teague—all have written or been written about.
- In the bibliography, you will find some new and old "classics." Remember though, it is not just names and dates you're searching for. You will be seeking clues that reveal the influences of the time and age. In this way, you can solve the mystery of why buildings, products, clothing and the like were designed to appear as they did.

DESIGN
Challenge

(From: *A Pattern Language*, Alexander et al., Oxford University Press, 1977. Reprinted with permission.)

STUDIO PLAN

On a beautiful day in early spring you walk up a steep slope into the woods to a small plot of land cleared of small trees. The sky is open above, clear and blue. The land is yours. And on this land, you will build your personal design studio.

From sharecropper shacks in the South to ice-fishing cabins on frozen northern lakes to manned space capsules, designers have been fascinated with the idea of creating small spaces that serve specific needs. Even trailers and campers express this interest in portable form.

Planning for a single purpose is no less difficult than building on a larger scale. The focus changes from "what must I absolutely include" to "what can I most easily do without." Prior to starting this type of construction project, you first have to list the tasks that will be performed in the space.

Then you must determine what objects will be needed to accomplish those tasks. The last step is to arrange the objects within the physical space. Or you might arrange them first, and then design the shape of the space around them. Let's remember that this is not merely an interior, it is a complete shelter and must provide some degree of human protection and facilities.

The site on which you will construct the studio, where you will practice the art and science of architecture, is in the upper Midwest. You are going to use it year round. You must think about electricity for your computer. Single use spaces like this will not exceed 168 square feet. A limited budget is available, and the site is somewhat remote.

The finished plan should be to scale so that materials could be purchased and shipped. One person should be able to build it. Congratulations and good luck.

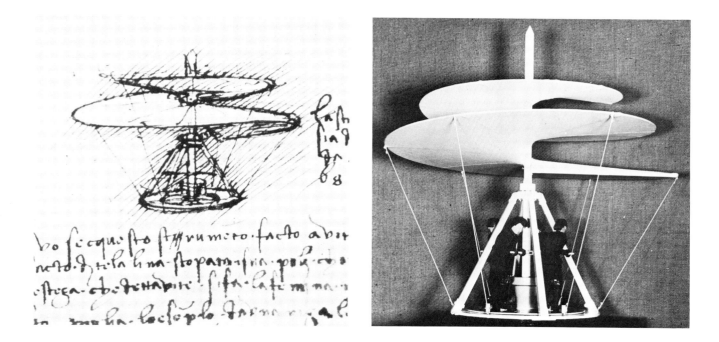

Who better than Leonardo Da Vinci to demonstrate inventive genius. Here's the helicopter, a bit before the twentieth century — 600 years or so. (Courtesy of IBM)

Museums

• Museums breathe design history. In even the humblest museum, you can find artifacts that show you "up close and personal" what a certain period was like. Some museum displays are arranged by time, showing a whole period at once. Other displays follow the history of something — perhaps even our toaster.

• The Smithsonian Institution in Washington, D. C. is a good example of a cultural and technological museum — some say the best. It is a living encyclopedia of the human quest for progress. Not to be missed are Air and Space Museum, the Centennial Exhibition Hall — in fact, try to see everything. A few days spent in these buildings not only will describe American history, but will also feed your interest and award you with inspiration and research of the most immediate and powerful kind.

POPULAR REFERENCE

• Another name for "popular reference" could be "informal" reference, because it refers to references you gather first-hand from your personal experience. You look, examine and develop connections of related or unrelated things to bring important information to your design solution. Sources of popular reference range from magazines — not design magazines — to a magic show.

• Let's recall the emergency shelter problem.

• There are some formal references that might prove helpful: tables that describe the strength of cardboard, books about simple architecture from other cultures (like igloos and teepees), plans for structures made out of plywood or fabric and wire. Even the drawings of Renaissance artist Leonardo Da Vinci might give you ideas for the shelter.

Let's see what's out there

• But this problem has few direct precedents in history. You might be better off if you went for a walk in the woods and checked out some really terrific ideas from animal architects. Birds, beaver, foxes and insects all construct their

Raymond Loewy
(American, 1893–1986)

Loewy virtually created the industrial design profession in the United States and showed how styling could help successful marketing. From the Coca-Cola bottle to the streamlined S-1 locomotive for the Pennsylvania Railroad, his designs were elegant and powerful.

After working as a window dresser, fashion illustrator and commercial artist, he set up an office in 1929. His first design, the Gestetner duplicating machine, led to commissions for a Coldspot refrigerator for Sears and the Pepsodent toothpaste dispenser. His designs were so impressive that the Museum of Modern Art produced a full-scale mock-up of his office in 1947. The classic Greyhound bus with its stylized dog symbol was one of his most memorable designs. The Studebaker Avanti, first built in 1962 and still in limited production today, secured Loewy's reputation as a pioneer of design.

March 3, 1936. Raymond Loewy and the mighty S-1 locomotive. Quite a change from the old model in the background. His rendering denotes speed by blurring the wheels. (Courtesy the Bettmann Archives)

homes from indigenous (found at the site) materials. Species like turtles and armadillos who have a plated or bony exoskeleton could tell you something.

• Maybe you could go for a walk on the beach and look at shells. Go to a kindergarten class and watch kids at play. See how they stack blocks, moving the elements around with great freedom. Talk to an engineer, a city planner, the lumberyard foreman — anyone who might connect to the problem.

• Use the people around you, also. Maybe your grandfather was a sailor. He may know how to pull rope so tightly it could hold the cardboard panels together.

Black Widow, a stabile, or standing mobile, by Alexander Calder. 1959, sheet metal, 7' 8'' by 14' 3''. (Courtesy of The Museum of Modern Art, New York. Mrs. Simon Guggenheim Fund)

Turn the concept around

• Begin to see the shelter as a container or a vessel and other sources for ideas will come into play. Get a lot of different cardboard containers — shoeboxes, perfume packages, food cartons — and break them down flat. Reassemble them differently. Go to a carpet retailer and get the cardboard centers from a used up carpet rolls. Toilet paper rolls are good, too.

• Go look at sculpture in a museum, gallery or art park, particularly large environmental metal stuff by artists like Mark DiSuvero, Kenneth Snelson and Alexander Calder.

• In other words, do your own leg work. Do you think it sounds a bit like brainstorming? Well, in a way, its action-brainstorming.

*Early bike versus
Mountain bike.
Revolution or evolution?*

PUTTING DESIGN IN CONTEXT

• In gathering reference, whether formal or popular, you are seeking to put your design in a context. You want to give it meaning in its own time, but understand how it fits into the big picture for all times. Some objects (like the compact disk player) arc so new, they have no historical reference. In that case, you either relate it to similar objects (stereo equipment), or you create a whole new design style or vernacular that defines the object as something radical.

• The evolution of the bicycle from the unsteady monster of the 1890s to the alloy-framed, twenty-speed racing bikes of today was an evolution. It was a gradual change brought about by technology. On the other hand, the Nike Air 180 running shoe and the Tizio lamp were more revolutionary. To challenge the future we must know where we come from.

Richard Sapper's design for Artemide became the Tizio lamp. This is a task light, with a transformer in the base powering a small halogen bulb that creates natural daylight. But it's the counter-balancing arms that have made it a classic design, so much so that there are dozens of imitators. (Courtesy of Artemide, Inc.)

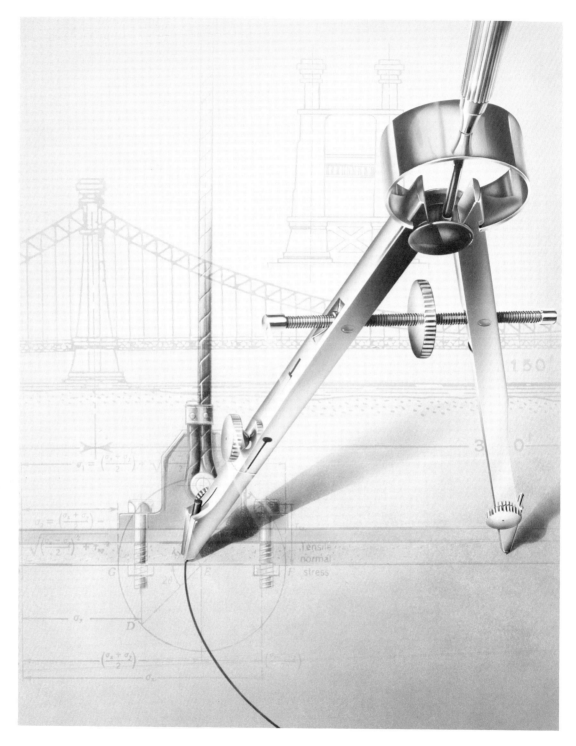

Drawing communicates the solution to the construction of this suspension bridge. (Courtesy of STN International)

Design is a LIVING process,

a series of adjustments, where the parts of the process — thinking and communicating — are inseparable. But in any book about design, the author has to divide these parts so that each can be made clearer. Bear in mind though, that just because a designer has put an idea down on paper or on a computer screen, it doesn't mean that the thinking time is over. Drawing, any kind of drawing, is a on-going conversation between the creator and the audience.

God is in the Details
— *Mies van de Rohe*

PUTTING DESIGN TO THE TEST

• In the earlier chapters, we focused on what design is, how we think about it, how it is done and why it is important. We used words like *think, conceive, invent*. Now that we understand the nature of design, it is time to enter into the world of communication. Here we use words like *see, visualize* and *describe*.

John and Washington Roebling's Brooklyn Bridge of 1883: possibly the most beautiful suspension span in the world. The Gothic arches piercing the towers and the spiderlike webbing of the cables are in sharp contrast to more modern bridge designs. (Photo by Wayne Andrews)

Getting your ideas into view

• Design solutions are put to the test when you finally get them down. After all, what good is an idea if you can't get it out where people can see it? Whether a drawing is quick and rough, or richly detailed and accurate, the point is that it gets an idea out of your head and into sight.

• Can you imagine trying to tell an engineer about the cable pattern in the Brooklyn Bridge, or talking about the shape of a new sports car without a picture to describe it ? A group of words is never enough, particularly since language is imprecise and open to different meanings.

Drawing is a learned skill

• The student generally says at this point, "Yes, but if you can't draw well, nobody will understand your idea." Well, naturally, the quality of your drawing is important. But you can learn to draw — and draw well enough to express your ideas with clarity and power.

- Drawing is a description of the object as it is and will be. It represents reality. But it is also an illusion, for we live in a three-dimensional world of length, width and depth. (Four, if you count time) A drawing is a flat, two-dimensional representation of the object, not the object itself. Because it is an illusion, a drawing expresses the *idea* of dimensions, not the actual dimensions. (For a three-dimensional representation, you would build a model.)
- The great thing about drawing is that it can communicate both ideas and emotions. People will get as excited about your solution as you are, if you can learn the skills to render your ideas well.

A COMMUNICATIONS SCALE

- "Drawing" is a catch-all word that is somewhat misleading. We call most pictorial images "drawings." But a drawing is also a type of graphic communication. In the graphic design profession, there is a scale or a hierarchy that helps to organize the drawing process.
- Remember that we are talking about a type of communication, not fine art. Our drawings are meant to be descriptions of designed objects. They are intended for other design professionals, rather than the general public. Rarely will designers be in a position to display their drawings as artwork. Even a magnificent watercolor rendering of a townhouse

development at sunset has little meaning outside of the circle of developers, architects, engineers and financial backers for the project.
- But your drawings are very important to that closed set of professionals — the engineers, architects, industrial designers, advertising people, craftspersons, modelmakers and anyone else — who must approve of or construct the finished piece. The following section describes the scale that designers use to present their ideas.

TYPES OF GRAPHIC COMMUNICATION

- Let's briefly run through each type of visual or graphic communication. Later, we'll investigate, show examples and explore each one in more detail.

Sketches

- This is the first and quickest form of graphic communication. A sketch is an idea frozen on paper. It is that first burst of creative energy that might present a usable element for a solution. It is visual thinking. Sketches can be very small doodles, referred to as thumbnails, or very large "concept" images. In the graphic design field, as in advertising, sketches are called "roughs."
- A designer should regard sketches the same way he regards brainstorming: every idea is legitimate. When you sketch, get every

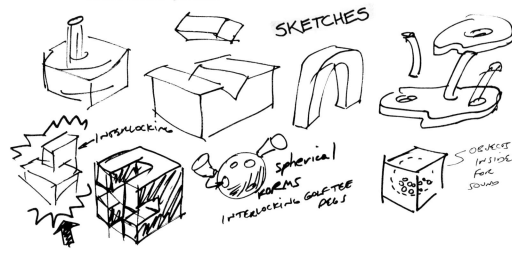

CHILDREN'S BLOCKS

SKETCHES

INTERLOCKING

spherical FORMS

INTERLOCKING GOLF-TEE PEGS

OBJECTS INSIDE FOR SOUND

idea down, and make as many drawings as you can. Sketches can be very, very powerful tools for communication. Because they are quick and rough, they contain the creative energy that explodes out of you when you are thinking. Some architects and designers, especially those regarded as geniuses, often go no further. They do a few sketches, each containing a dynamic image about the design concept. Then others work up the sketches into more finished drawings.

Drawings

• Because we use the word "drawing" in a general sense, as I mentioned earlier, it can be confusing. Technically, however, a drawing is the stage of graphic communication after sketching. A drawing is a more finished image than a sketch. It is generally more detailed or accurate.

• Often, a designer will examine a bunch of sketches and then decide to polish up just a few. You might combine parts of one with parts of another, edit and re-draw the object. Because a drawing is less rough and more studied than a sketch, it is easier for a non-professional to understand.

Technical Drawing

• In the industrial/manufacturing business, technical drawings (or working drawings) are accurate, dimensioned and scaled drawings that describe an object with precision. If you've seen blueprints, you've seen technical drawings. They are what a draftsman draws, what a machinist measures, what a contractor orders lumber from.

• Courses that teach technical drawing techniques are usually called "mechanical drawing," because you need special tools to ensure accuracy. And because things are manufactured or constructed based on these drawings, they have to be drawn in a special way, with special rules. In that way, everyone involved in the process can understand them. Depending on the object — a house, a car, a radio, product packaging — different types of working drawings might be needed.

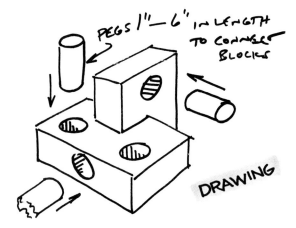

PEGS 1"—6" IN LENGTH TO CONNECT BLOCKS

DRAWING

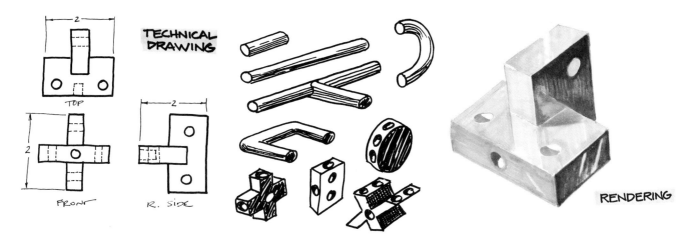

TECHNICAL DRAWING

TOP

FRONT

R. SIDE

RENDERING

- There are six generally recognized types of technical drawing: orthographic projections; auxiliary views; revolutions; section views; developments and transitions; and pictorial drawings.

- A designer will decide which types of technical drawings are needed to describe the object. For instance, maybe you have designed a set of interlocking building blocks for preschool children. You would want to show a manufacturer each type of block in all three dimensions — length, width and depth. The best type of technical drawing to describe the block would be an orthographic projection, because it shows three sides. If, however, the block has an angled surface, one that is not at a right angle, you might add an auxiliary view to describe the inclined surface.

- Technical drawings show the dimensions of the object and are drawn to scale. They are a common language among designers, manufacturers, craftspeople and tradespeople. Although they can be quite interesting to look at, their most important qualities are accuracy and clarity.

Rendering

- A rendering is a dramatized presentation of your design. It serves a number of purposes. Since it is a stylized or artistically drawn image, it can be a convincing sales tool. You can use a rendering to show off a design to its best advantage. It can be emotive: adding a sunset and frolicking people in front of those new houses you are designing not only will help attract buyers, but might also convince a bank to lend you the money to build more.

- Often in full color, a rendering most closely approaches the idea of fine art. Because it is an illustration, it takes certain liberties with dimensions and accuracy in order to be dramatic. The best renderings are often hung on the walls of the architect's office or above the client's desk as a proud reminder of a successful project.

Both architects and designers need to express their ideas in three dimensions. Many structures, as in this city plan, must be viewed in relationship to each other.

Models

• As we said earlier, a drawing gives an illusion of three dimensions on a flat, two-dimensional surface. A model is actually three-dimensional. The advantage of building a model is to more closely approximate the final object. Some models, such as automobile models, are made full-sized. But most models are made small enough to sit on a table top. You can make a rough model (often called a form or volume model), or a highly finished model, (a presentation model). The advantage of a model over a drawing is that you can examine the form over its entire surface. You can pick it up, walk around it and even reform it. You can feel how it fits in the hand.

• The disadvantages of models are also considerable. Model building is a time-consuming process. You need a shop space and, often, very specialized skills. In fact, most architects send their working drawings and renderings to professional, full-time modelmakers.

This model for automobile design will be tested in a wind tunnel and observed from every angle so both its appearance and efficiency can be determined. As these designers carve the model, they refer to full size drawing and smaller sketches in the background. (Courtesy of GM)

unusual to see hundreds of quick images produced by a creative team in response to a logotype problem. Once the final few are chosen, they make a comprehensive (or comp), which is like a drawing. Finally a mechanical is prepared. That is a final technical drawing of the logo, ready for the printing process.

• Keep in mind that the visualization process is a dialogue between you and your ideas, and between you and your audience. That audience might be co-designers, your boss, the client, a sales team, the engineering department, the shop foreman, a machinist, a weaver — anyone who has to understand your concept and how it will be made. The audience determines what types of visuals will be needed.

Where do you start?

• Before we practice any of these methods, it is important to understand a few basic ideas at the heart of the visualization experience. It might seem that, to successfully complete a design project, you have to complete some sketches, turn them into a drawing, then a technical drawing, then a rendering and finally a model.

• That's not necessarily true.

• For one project, all you might need are a few sketches. For another, you might present a drawing, then construct a model, then take measurements from the model and use them to finalize a technical drawing as a blueprint. Industrial designers frequently use clay as a sketching material, forming the object by physically tearing and twisting, squeezing and melding

until an exciting image grows out of it. Architects sketch floor plans, then do the elevations for each of the outside walls. Sometimes they construct a volume or form model out of foam core board, just to get a feel for the scale and visual weight of the building.

• No one creates more roughs than graphic designers. It's not

Teamwork is often a great way to solve complex problems. Defending your solutions takes good visual and verbal communications skills.

- How well you choose the method of communication as well as the clarity and flair of your artistic expression are both important. They demonstrate your ability to complete a design project. That's why a designer's education is heavily weighted toward visual expression.

DRAWING FROM LIFE — THE FOUNDATION SKILL

- There are two sources for drawing: imagination and real life. Okay, these are big categories. But it brings up an important point. When you imagine a solution to a problem, your drawings must communicate your image clearly. But it's your dream and you own the image. Others have to understand what you have created, true, but you invented it so it can look unreal, unusual, however you like. Often it is supported by additional notes.
- When you draw from life, you base the work on observation. You are speaking in a language that is obvious. Anyone should be able to understand the results.
- Can you approach both drawing processes the same way?
- No, I don't think so. From early childhood, you have absorbed thousands of visual reference points. You have built a vocabulary of images. When you draw from the imagination, you use forms and shapes learned in previous observations. The brain reassembles them into new patterns.

- How do you refresh and sharpen this vocabulary? By drawing from life. By observing and recording. Although designers use both types of working processes — imaginative drawing and life drawing — I'm convinced that you can't communicate well unless you learn to see. You have to observe and then learn to record, to draw. So the first drawing skill every designer needs is the ability to draw from life.

The 3 essentials

- Even before a designer starts to sketch, even before brainstorming possible answers to a problem, a designer arms himself with three basic essentials.

Be willing to accept failure
- The first one is the acceptance of failure. That's right — floppo city. You know why?
- Because you're going to mess up on most of your drawings, especially if you are a student. Not only will some of your ideas miss the mark (which they should if you're probing enough), but the quality of the drawings will be infantile and silly.
- Most people communicate better verbally than visually for a simple reason: they do it all the time. Humans crave the sound of other voices and relish the chance to share in a discussion. When folks stop talking or singing, they get rusty pipes and clogged

brains. Their vocabulary gets weak. They lose the ability to express themselves clearly and accurately.
- All kids love to draw, but most stop around the sixth grade when they realize that their skills no longer capture the true image of something. As adults, they do not observe and visually record in detail what is around them. After all, they can express themselves in words, right? Since designers must communicate visually, they have to redevelop those skills abandoned as a child.
- It's difficult and painful to feel so anxious and so inept. So be prepared to fail. But if you keep practicing, you can achieve what I call visual literacy.

Keep a visual diary
- In order to achieve visual literacy, you need a sketchbook. This is your proving ground, your experimental station, your hidden diary of visual images.
- Now start to draw from life. All you need is a pencil, or charcoal, or a pen, or a felt tip marker. Learn to look, to observe common objects with a keen eye. You don't have to search out grand themes like the park on a wintry day. A fork will do nicely. A lamp is good. Or the instrument panel of a car. There are many comprehensive books on drawing. All of them offer methods that

DESIGN
Challenge

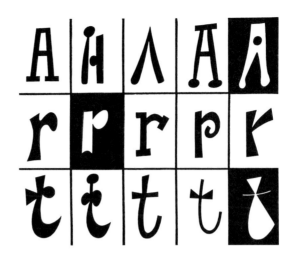

LETTERFORMS

Understanding and using typography (letterforms) is an essential part of graphic design. Letters, type, are as important to design as color is to a painter, good wood to a cabinetmaker. Preferences in typestyles have changed a lot over the years. Thousands of fonts, or type families, have been created by individual designers. Different typefaces convey different feelings and attitudes. Some are stuffy and look formal — like those commonly found in textbooks. Others are less formal, even playful. Examples of these can be seen in advertising, especially "young" products.

The ability to use letters and images together is the basic foundation of visual design. By relating two graphic elements, a letter and a symbol, a new idea can be created.

Take, for example, a heart and the letter H. If you were to use just these two images and add a background element, you could tell many stories. A fat, heavy, block capital H with a rip down the center and the edge of a heart emerging, set against a background of graph lines, might tell the story of a broken heart. What message is sent by many small, delicate lower case h's falling into a hole in the ground shaped like a heart. Ouch!

When you manipulate letters and simple images, you can express your personal vision. You can communicate your own feelings about an idea, emotion or political belief. Choose a letter and an image. Place them in a background and communicate. Look at many typestyles. Do whatever you want to the image: change it, stretch it, flatten it, poke holes in it. Make a lot of thumbnails and then test them out on other people. See if the message you send is the message they receive.

can help you improve. Find one that speaks clearly to you. Maybe a design instructor could get you started with a favorite.

• The point is: to learn to draw, you have to draw. Period. Then, when your imagination comes knocking, you'll be confident that you can express yourself clearly.

Understand the basic elements and principles

• The third essential for every designer is to understand of the elements of design and the principles of art. Drawing is a visual activity. If your drawings are going to express your ideas in a clear and dynamic way, it's vital that you understand the basic principles of visual communication. Art is a language that we all speak and one that has been spoken to us. Some people run from art because they think they lost, or never had, the ability to be good at it.

• That's nonsense.

• In the arts there are simple rules that can be used to improve the quality of the images you make. The more you know, the better you'll get at using artistic principles to achieve your communication and design goals.

THE ELEMENTS OF DESIGN

• There are six basic elements to design:

  ✔ Line
  ✔ Shape
  ✔ Form
  ✔ Space
  ✔ Texture
  ✔ Color

• That's the total list. You're probably are familiar with most of them already. So it's really just a matter of learning how they work to make your visual expression as effective as possible.

Line

• Line, of course, is the most basic element. A line is a two-dimensional mark connecting two points that starts and ends without crossing over itself. A line can be thin or fat, broken or smooth, straight or curved or in any combination of these.

Drawing tools

• Different drawing tools make different types of line or linear qualities. Pencils come in a range of hardness, rated from very soft, 6B, to very, very hard, 6H. A hard pencil makes a clean, crisp line, even if you bear down. A soft pencil can start a line as a fine light mark, but as you continue to draw you can gradually press down to make the line fat, dark and soft. As you release pressure, the line remains wide but it turns grey. A felt-tip pen or fine-line marker generally makes a mark that is even in weight (darkness) and thickness. But if you press hard on a fiber tip pen, it will splay out and soften the line and the color. It has been said that ink is the cosmetic

line

PENCIL

MARKER, FELT TIP

BRUSH

TECHNICAL PEN

line

↑ CALM

EMOTIONAL ↓

• HORIZONTAL •
CALM, STATIC

• VERTICAL •
STABLE STRONG

• DIAGONAL •
DYNAMIC, TENSION

that ideas wear when they go out in public; graphite (pencils) are their dirty truth.

• A technical pen is a fixed-size, permanent ink instrument. Each technical pen point makes one thickness of line in a solid weight. You can change line thickness by changing the point. A brush is just the opposite. Brushes offer the widest range of linear effects. One brush can go from swooping, curved, heavy strokes to wispy, thin, watery lines. It can be the most expressive and free of all drawing instruments. This expressiveness is particularly important in renderings, where you want to be as expressive and emotional as possible.

• Using a CAD (Computer-Assisted Drafting) program, allows you to choose any line thickness to make straight and curved lines. Geometric forms are its specialty. A computer, however, has a tough time varying the thickness and weight of a single line. It cannot make a smooth change from thin to thick, dark to light, within one mark. Nevertheless, CAD remains the best tool to construct working drawings where lines are the most frequently used element.

• Where CAD falls short is in making renderings, where gradual and subtle effects are needed. Currently, only the most powerful supercomputers are capable of manipulating the information needed to prepare an effective and interesting rendering.

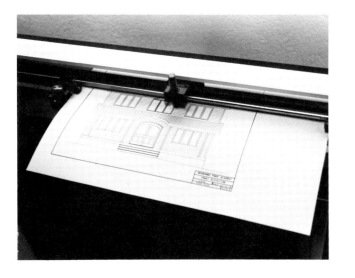

When using a computer, your drawing is usually from a plotter equipped with a variety of pen sizes. You can control the lines as you draw them (input) or later during the plotting (output).

Shape

• Shape is the element that describes what happens when a line crosses over itself. Once you enclose a two-dimensional space, you have constructed a shape of length and width. Shapes are either geometric or natural. Rectangular, triangular or circular shapes are geometric or human-made elements. Natural shapes, also called organic shapes, are irregular and free-form. When you look at the designed environment, you will notice some objects made up of geometric shapes and others that are more organic.

• Earlier we talked about the designs of Luigi Colani (p. 56). His work demonstrates his belief that humans relate best to organic shapes and forms. Other designers, for example the Bauhaus school in pre-World War II Germany and the architect Mies van de Rohe, preferred the cool logic and hard edges of geometry in their work.

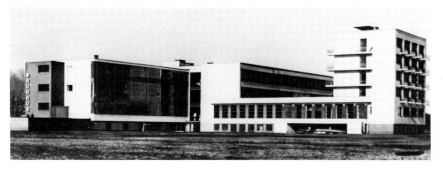

The Bauhaus, a pre-WW II design institute in Germany, taught clean, cool and hard-edged architecture, product and graphic design. You can see it reflected in these structures.

GEOMETRIC SHAPES

NATURAL SHAPES

SYMBOLIC

EMOTIONAL

• Lately, designers are less willing to be locked into one style or the other. They prefer to choose freely from a dictionary of shapes in order to answer specific problems.

Form

• Form is the three-dimensional representation of shape. Adding depth gives the object a physical presence. Not only can you see it, you can pick it up or walk around it. A form has weight and takes up space.

• The descriptions of geometric and organic shapes also apply to forms. With the exception of graphic design which generally remains in two dimensions, most design efforts end up in a constructed or fabricated three-dimensional form.

• Some designers feel that since the finished object will be a form, they should sketch in three dimensions. That's why car designers make clay models and architects make volume models.

Frank Lloyd Wright
(American, 1869–1959)

Probably the most famous American architect, Wright began his career in Chicago in 1888. His first house in Oak Park, Illinois, was followed by a series of unique residences which came to be known as "Prairie" style. The design featured long, low horizontals with wide overhangs and shallow roofs, brick and stone. The effect was a structure that appeared to lie close to the ground. He insisted that interiors be fully integrated spaces and often designed the furniture, lights, stained glass and other fittings.

He was heavily influenced by Japanese design, as well as by late nineteenth-century English buildings of Voysey. His most powerful design was the Edgar Kaufmann house, "Falling Water," in Bear Run, Pennsylvania. It's a dramatic combination of a unique site — a stream falling from a rock outcrop — and a design calculated to take advantage of the setting. His commercial structures include the Larkin Building in Buffalo, New York, the Imperial Hotel in Tokyo, Japan, the Johnson Wax building in Racine, Wisconsin, and the Guggenheim Museum in New York City. They were all original inspirations, the first of their kind.

Falling Water — a Frank Lloyd Wright icon. (Courtesy of the Frank Lloyd Wright Foundation)

Space

• Space is the area displaced by a shape or form. It's what's left after you draw shapes on paper or put a model in a box. Think of it as the background. In fact, it is often called negative space.

• We have a tendency to think of space as something that's just there surrounding everything else. Actually, space is the element that defines most architecture problems. The final shape of an exterior is formed by the edges of the building — the roof line, the side edges and the ground line. Placed against the background of the sky and the earth, we see the object. Those edges describe where one shape (the building) leaves off and the larger shape (the space) takes over.

• Inside a home, for example, an architect divides space into usable areas we call rooms. Each can have a special function, but the dimensions of each space often tell us what the "feel" of the home will be like. How you choose to furnish each space, how you populate it with other forms, is based as much on the spaces between objects as the objects themselves.

• There is no doubt that a designer has to be concerned with space as much as with form. Space is not just what's left over. It's a basic feature of every design.

An indoor mall for mixed-use. The spaces are divided horizontally and vertically. (Courtesy of the Onandaga County Public Library)

Texture

• Texture refers to the surface of an object. An object can be drawn to look rough or smooth. If the object is a form, it will have a tactile quality; you will be able to feel the texture. These two types of texture are called visual and physical texture.

• Designers are aware of the appeal of texture. Manipulating the surface of an object — making it shiny and sleek or nubby and dull — gives the piece an emotional quality. Textures are often planned at the same time as the final form of an object. For they work best when considered together. Like form and space, you can't do one without affecting the other. A lot of design today is monochromatic, one color. Because the color is so simple, the texture becomes even more important. New materials, particularly plastics and resins, give the designer a lot of choices for giving object a special feel.

Color

- Color is the designer's most powerful tool. It is a complex element. Humor, playfulness, drama, flash and seriousness are just some of the effects that color can create.

What is color?

- The color we see, of course, is caused by light reflecting off a surface. The intensity of light affects the intensity of the color. Colors are called *hues*; the power or purity of a color is called its *chroma* or *value*.
- Most people remember the primary colors (red, blue and yellow) and the secondary colors (orange, violet and green). These colors are common to the additive scale. Yellow, cyan and magenta are part of a color system called subtractive and are used in printing. If you look closely at a photo or a color illustration in a magazine, you can see it is made up of tiny dots of subtractive color, plus black. Video images, on television and computer screens, are made up of dots (called phosphors) of red, green and blue (additive colors). The intensity of the color depends on the strength of an electron beam that strikes the phosphors from the rear of the screen.

The emotional impact of color

- Designers need to be aware of the emotional impact of color. This can be as simple as the idea of red being a warm color. But colors have also been given meaning by society: red is the color of danger, fire engines and stop signs. In our society, white means purity; in the Orient it's associated with death.
- Architects often decide color schemes for houses based on what is traditional for that part of the country. Homes in "colonial" New England are painted soft blues, reds and muted tones. In Florida, bright white, pink, turquoise and intense hues are the norm. Automobile designers can also break down preferences by region. They know which color cars will sell best in the West, the South, etc.
- Although you can sketch in color, generally it is added at the rendering stage of design. The basic forms and textures are worked out first. Then color is added to give emotional punch to the rendering. Markers, colored pencil, watercolors, acrylic paints and airbrush are typical mediums for putting color into a visual presentation.

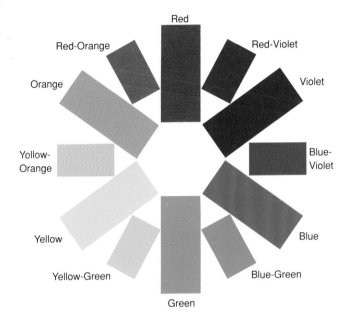

Here are the additive colors: primary, secondary as well as mixtures of the two called tertiary colors.

Using a magnifying glass, you can see combinations of these four subtractive colors (also called process colors) in all printed color photographs.

Yellow

Cyan

Magenta

Black

Pastel colors (purples, pinks, blues, greens) dominate this album and CD cover. Why is it that these colors make us think of rain forests and oceans? What words might describe these colors? Gentle? Warm? Soft breezes? (Design and illustration by Susan Marsh. Courtesy of Rounder Records)

COMPUTER-AIDED DESIGN

Computer-aided design (CAD) promotes experimentation and change. Most designers still prefer to work with traditional materials during the concept stage. But as computers grow more powerful and friendly, perhaps paper and pencil will fade way. (Courtesy of the New York Institute of Design; and, below, Baudville, Grand Rapids, Michigan)

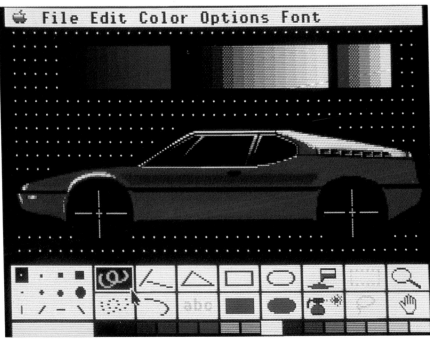

This experimental hybrid aircraft — part plane, part helicopter — has the smooth sculptural forms possible with modern composite materials. It flies like a helicopter at speeds up to 215 mph. Then the "X-wing" locks in place, and this strange bird travels like an airplane at speeds up to 600 mph. (Courtesy of NASA)

Here's a light with a sense of humor. You can manipulate it into human or animal forms. Is this a good marketing feature? I wonder what the design brief looked like. (Courtesy of Eddy Light)

FURNITURE

The Icarus Chair by Stephen Daniell blends craft and mythology, demonstrating the far reaches of contemporary furniture. (Courtesy of Moira James Gallery)

This plywood — yes, plywood — LCM chair by Charles Eames proves that machine-made objects can have an organic feel. (Courtesy of Herman Miller, Inc.)

Textiles offer the designer an opportunity to create patterns in both geometric and natural forms. These are printed on or woven into fabric to make richly textured material. (Courtesy of Collier Campbell Textiles)

We wear hats to be silly or suave, to keep the rain out of our hair and the sun off our face. Hat designers play with color, shape and texture to achieve the desired effect. Like most design, it's a question of form and function.

ARCHITECTURE

The futurist architect Antonio Sant'Elia produced this color rendering for his Inner City project. The date — 1914! Like other futurists, Sant'Elia envisioned a world dominated by technology. (Marcherita G. Sarfatti Collection, Rome)

The dramatic design of architect Frank Gehry's California Aerospace Museum in Los Angeles shows that even block-like forms can give off a sense of energy. The jet aircraft adds a feeling of dynamic power and speed. (Photo by Michael Moran)

It's just the number 9: you've seen it thousands of times. But this sculpture by Ivan Chermayeff identifies a place — 9 West 57th Street in New York City — and has become a locator...like, "Meet me at the 9 at ten." (Photo by David Robbins)

GRAPHIC DESIGN

Powerful images make a lasting point and stay in your memory for a long time. The toe-shoe and walnut almost become an exclamation point as well as a play of soft against hard. (Courtesy of Kauck Photography, Inc.)

The Cincinnati Ballet Company Presents the

NUTCRACKER

Music Hall
December 21-30
Five matinees and
five evening
performances

This production is
sponsored by
Frisch's Restaurants, Inc.

CINCINNATIBALLET
David McLain, Artistic Director

THE PRINCIPLES OF ART

• The principles of art are not laws, but a way to help you control the elements of design. They help make your images, your pictorial expression, clear and organized. Once you can make these principles work for you, you can control the effect of your design and influence the way people react to your work.

• The principles of art are:

✔ Balance
✔ Pattern and repetition
✔ Rhythm
✔ Movement
✔ Emphasis
✔ Unity

Balance

• Balance is visual equality. In a drawing, it refers to how you organize what's on the page. In every work of art, there is a point of focus. It might be the most detailed part of a drawing, or the most colorful, or the biggest single thing. If you want viewers to look at something in particular or look at it first, you can drive eyes to that thing by balancing or unbalancing the work.

• There are many ways to balance a design. You can organize the image on the page horizontally, where the objects are on the left and right hand sides. You can organize it vertically, where the images are balanced top and bottom. If you make the elements in equal portions, so that both sides match,

you have created symmetry. Symmetry creates a formal, structured feeling. If you unbalance your page, you have asymmetry or informality. Finally, if you have one central object and organize others around it, this is called radial balance. Radial designs are typical of flowers, snails and microscopic life forms.

Pattern and repetition

• When you use an image more than once in a composition, you create repetition. If you repeat it with regularity, you create pattern. They both have a strong visual impact and are often used by artists to link together parts of a picture. They also are used to give visual texture to drawings. If a designer wants to show a textured surface of an object, say the handle of a steam iron, he uses a pattern to suggest a change in visual texture from smooth to rough.

• A motif is a single piece of a pattern, the part that is repeated. Some patterns are random, for

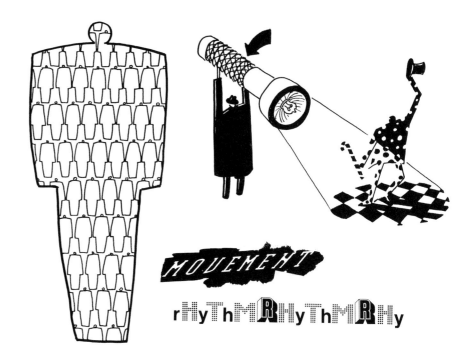

Attitudes of Animals in Motion, a series of photographs by Eadweard Muybridge, were of great interest to the scientific community in the late 1800s. This horse study illustrates the principles of rhythm and movement quite clearly. (Courtesy of Sotheby's, Inc., 1987)

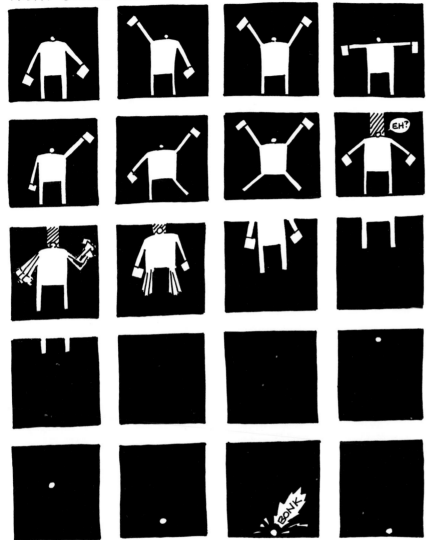

NIGHT SEMAPHORE SIGNALING BEFORE ALIEN ABDUCTION.

* DO NOT LOOK AT THIS IMAGE TOO LONG, LEST YOU BECOME HYPNOTIZED AND SEE GRAY DOTS.........

example, polka dots or footprints in the sand. A plaid is a pattern formed by a grid system. An alternating pattern is consistent but changing; a checkerboard, a brick wall, striped fabric all contain alternating patterns. Like radial balance, radial patterns repeat around a central image. Wood grain, hair and waves are examples of rhythmic pattern; rhythmic patterns are frequently found in natural objects.

Rhythm

• Rhythm is organized repetition. Images move to a beat in the composition. In a rhythmic pattern, the positive shapes and the negative spaces make a visual arrangement. Like a pattern, which is repetition you see, a rhythm is repetition you feel.

Movement

• Movement happens when a sequence produces a feeling or when the rhythm is in a sequence, similar to stop-action photography. When many similar or identical elements are used, you can set up a rhythmical or pulsating sequence. This can direct the viewer into following the overall image.

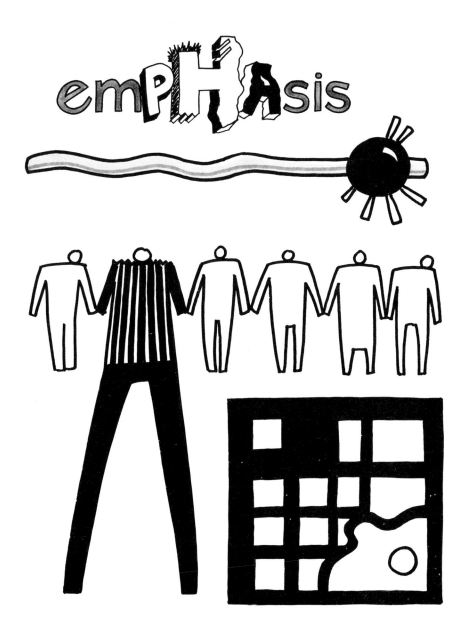

- Emphasis is a way to control or direct the viewer. When you emphasize one area. you make that area a focal point. You can create emphasis through contrast, by making a visible difference in size, color, texture or shape. A square in a sea of circles will draw your attention first. The careful placement of a key object will call attention to it, too.

Unity

• Unity is the principle that proves you have used the other principles. Unity means that it looks right and feels right. When a composition on a page, or a model in clay, or any other design is said to have unity, that means it feels complete. Although unity is a difficult thing to measure, the more you participate in creative design, the clearer it will become. Promise.

IF YOU WERE ASKED TO THINK ABOUT WHICH OF THESE TWO RADIOS WAS THE MORE STRONGLY UNIFIED DESIGN, WHICH WOULD YOU DEFEND AND WHY?

The high-technology sneaker. Although this is a technical drawing of the product, it retains a fresh, almost comedic sense, convincing you that this is a highly sophisticated, engineered product, but very cool, too. (Courtesy of Nike)

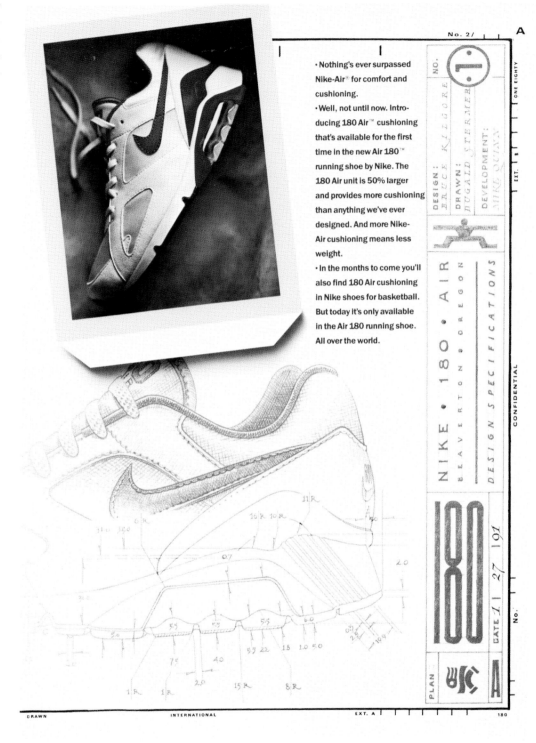

No. 27

A

- Nothing's ever surpassed Nike-Air® for comfort and cushioning.
- Well, not until now. Introducing 180 Air™ cushioning that's available for the first time in the new Air 180™ running shoe by Nike. The 180 Air unit is 50% larger and provides more cushioning than anything we've ever designed. And more Nike-Air cushioning means less weight.
- In the months to come you'll also find 180 Air cushioning in Nike shoes for basketball. But today it's only available in the Air 180 running shoe. All over the world.

DESIGN: BRUCE KILGORE
DRAWN: DUGALD STERMER
DEVELOPMENT: MIKE QUAN

ONE EIGHTY

EXT. B

NIKE · 180 · AIR
BEAVERTON · OREGON

DESIGN SPECIFICATIONS

CONFIDENTIAL

180

DATE 1 27 191

No.

PLAN

A

DRAWN   INTERNATIONAL   EXT. A   180

Everything

WE DESIGN

must be fabricated, constructed, formed, shaped, built, etc.

The artist possesses the ability to breathe soul into the lifeless product of the machine.
— Walter Gropius

We, as designers, develop the form of an object. But it is rare that we actually make the final object. Unless we are craftspersons, who design and make one-of-a-kind objects, many copies will be made of our original.

• If some one else will be making your design, how can you be sure that the design will turn out exactly as you had planned?

• Well, the answer is good communications between the creator, you, and the production person or persons — the manufacturer, builder or printer. For good communications, you need precise drawings. You need drawings that detail the object so it can be understood by everyone involved in the project.

THE LANGUAGE OF INDUSTRY

• During the Industrial Revolution in Great Britain, factories began to mass produce goods for industry

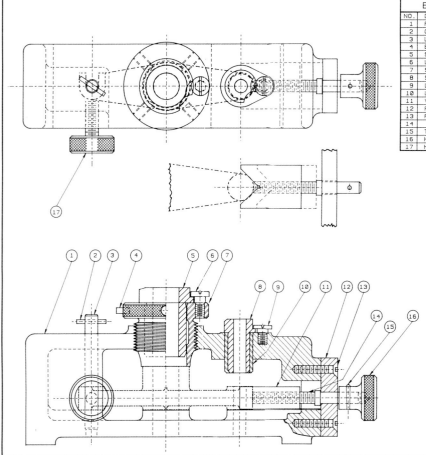

BILL OF MATERIALS

NO.	DESCRIPTION	MAT.	QTY	REMARKS
1	FRAME	C1	1	SEE DETAILS
2	CROSS PIN	CRS	1	1/8D X 1 1/8
3	LOCATING PIN	CRS	1	7/16D X 3 5/8
4	BUSHING PIN	CRS	4	3/16D X 3/8
5	SLIP BUSHING	PURCH	1	UNIVER. ENG A75
6	LOCK SCREW		1	DO NO.2
7	SCR. BUSHING	SAE1112	1	SEE DETAILS
8	SLIP BUSHING	PURCH	1	UNIVER. ENG A73
9	LOCK SCREW		1	DO NO.1
10	LIN. BUSHING		1	DO NO.53
11	V BLOCK	SAE1020	1	SEE DETAILS
12	PLATE	SAE1030	1	DO
13	FLAT HD. SCR.	STD	2	5/16-18NC 1 1/4
14	OLLAR SCR.	SAE1112	1	SEE DETAILS
15	TAPER PIN	CRS	1	NO. 000
16	HAND WHEEL	CRS	1	SEE DETAILS
17	HAND SCR.	SAE1112	1	DO

and consumers. Three people became involved in the making of a single object: the designer, who created it; the manufacturing engineer, who figured out how to make it; and the person (usually a machine operator) who actually made the object. They needed a system, so that the design could be clearly communicated to everyone. This system became known as mechanical or technical drawing.

• Technical drawing was taught in schools and universities, and to tradespeople on the job. Because it had to be clearly understood by everyone, a standard set of instructions, rules and drawing types developed and were used by everyone. The industrialization of Europe and, later, the United States could not have happened without this system of universal communication, which is still called the "language of industry."

• The rules of technical drawing are called drawing conventions and they are still in use today. And since your product will most likely end up being made by someone else, it is important for you to know how to communicate this

way. A well-drawn technical drawing is more accurate and often provides a clearer, more detailed description of an object than a photograph or a page of notes.

• The following information about this important aspect of design is brief. It does not go into great detail. One reason is that this book is not strictly about technical drawing. Another reason is that Computer-Assisted Drawing (CAD) programs are rapidly eliminating the need for a lot of the more repetitive phases of technical drawing. However, whether you use traditional equipment or the computer, the drafting standards for shaping technical drawings remain unchanged.

The basic rules of technical drawings

• First, there are some elementary points that are true of all technical drawings:

• Precision, accuracy, detail and clarity are the most important concerns. All technical drawings must be clean and precise. You must accurately measure each element and label it with a dimension. Remember, engineers, machinists and building contractors will actually measure your lines to get the true size of a piece. If your measurements are off, theirs will be, too. Since you will put instructions and directions right on your drawings, your lettering must be clear. This means that you

have to develop a uniform alphabet and be consistent in using it.

Traditional tools

• If you will be working with traditional tools, you will have: a *T-square* for making parallel horizontal lines, *triangles* for vertical lines, a *compass* for circles and arcs, a *scale* for measuring your lines and shapes, a series of *pencils* ranging from hard lead (for laying out the position of your objects) to softer lead (for the finished object lines), an *eraser* and other specialized tools you might use in unusual situations.

• You will be drawing on a *board or table* that is smooth and free from dents and digs. Your paper will be held in place by *drafting tape* or *push pins*. The paper will be

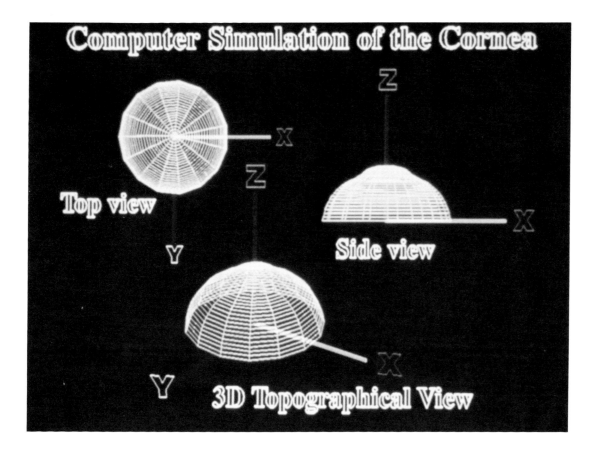

Computer Simulation of the Cornea

Top view

Side view

3D Topographical View

A drawing of the human cornea can spin in space thanks to computer design programs. (Courtesy of NASA)

squared up, that is, aligned to the edge of the board and the T-square. When the paper is aligned correctly, you know that every line will be parallel and at right angles, insuring that your objects will remain true to size and scale.

Designing on the computer

• Of course, CAD is completely different. With the most powerful computers, mainframes, you would be drawing at a work station. But most CAD operations are done on PCs or personal computers.

• Why use a computer? Well after the initial learning period, you can speed up the process of drafting by at least 40 percent. In addition, it is simple and fast to revise, or change, a drawing without having to redraw the entire sheet. The best CAD programs allow you to rotate the shapes you have created, show texture, light the object, automatically dimension the object, add views and even animate the sequence in which the object was developed and drawn. The more powerful computers can turn working drawings into full-color renderings.

Computer tools

• The work is displayed on a video screen (or monitor). Sometimes two screens are used: one for a menu of commands from which you can select an operation, the other for the image itself. You type in your lettering and give the computer commands on a keyboard in front of the screen. In addition, some computers have a "mouse." You can draw with the mouse and give directions to the computer, too.

• A digitizing tablet is an input device with a flat surface. You can draw directly on the tablet and the computer will "read" your drawings. Overlays or templates are available for the digitizer. These templates are linked to data stored in the computer, containing such information as door and window styles or screws and bolts. You can just point and click on a particular part, pictured on the template. The computer will automatically draw it in for you. If you give each part a price value, the computer will even add up the cost of materials for a particular job.

• In order to get a "hard copy" of your drawing you need an output device — a printer or, more likely, a plotter. A plotter is an electromechanical pen that draws the image as it receives information from the computer. Like traditional drawing paper plotters come in various sizes.

A Computer System

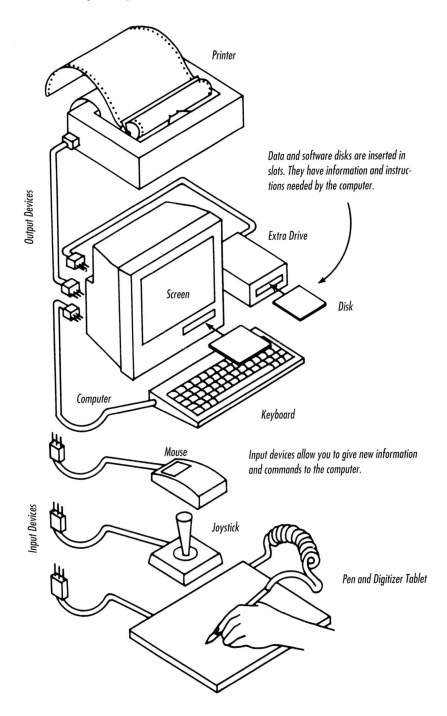

Printer

Data and software disks are inserted in slots. They have information and instructions needed by the computer.

Output Devices

Extra Drive

Disk

Screen

Computer

Keyboard

Input Devices

Mouse

Input devices allow you to give new information and commands to the computer.

Joystick

Pen and Digitizer Tablet

Can a computer give you more than you got?

• CAD systems can do many wonderful things for the designer. As prices come down and software becomes more and more "user friendly," you won't see too many traditional drafting outfits around. But remember this key rule about computers: *garbage in = garbage out*. It means that if you put in inaccurate information, that's exactly what you'll get out.

Conversing with the cannibals

• Sometimes designers and artists feel intimidated by technical drawing because it seems complex and steeped in rules. That's not really true. If you were traveling in a foreign country, you would need to know enough of the language to make yourself understood by the locals. But you don't have to be able to discuss the meaning of life with the taxicab driver. All you need is a few key words and phrases: "Take me to a hotel." "How much?" "I think you owe me some change."

• Think of technical drawing as the language of a foreign country. To get around, you just have to know the basics. Later, if you have a specialized need, you can learn a little more. A designer is a traveler who must learn enough language to communicate his design to the natives — and not get eaten in the process.

TECHNICAL DRAWING SWAT VISUALIZERS

"FRED"
ASSIGNMENT: TO GET VISUAL INFO FROM THE **FRONT**

"TINA"
ASSIGNMENT: TO OBTAIN VIEWS FROM THE **TOP**

"SUE"
ASSIGNMENT: TO GET **SIDE** VIEWS

"AL"
ASSIGNMENT: USED IN SUPPORT SITUATIONS TO GET HELPER VIEWS

ORTHOGRAPHIC VIEWING SYSTEM

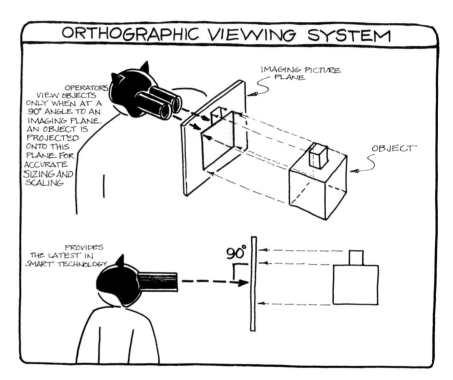

OPERATORS VIEW OBJECTS ONLY WHEN AT A 90° ANGLE TO AN IMAGING PLANE. AN OBJECT IS PROJECTED ONTO THIS PLANE FOR ACCURATE SIZING AND SCALING

IMAGING PICTURE PLANE

OBJECT

PROVIDES THE LATEST IN SMART TECHNOLOGY

90°

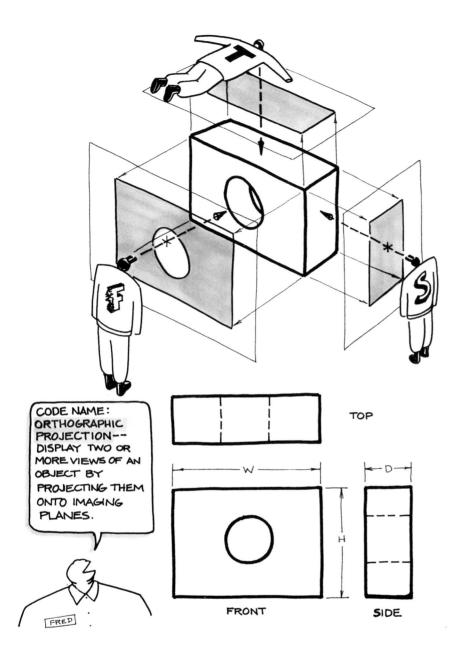

CODE NAME:
ORTHOGRAPHIC
PROJECTION--
DISPLAY TWO OR
MORE VIEWS OF AN
OBJECT BY
PROJECTING THEM
ONTO IMAGING
PLANES.

FRED

TOP

W

H

FRONT

D

SIDE

BASIC TECHNICAL DRAWING TYPES

• In technical drawing, you must always imagine that your sheet of paper or your screen is a flat piece of transparent material. We call it the picture plane. Everything we want to measure accurately has to be up against the picture plane. So, the most elementary principle behind this type of drawing is simply that we must move objects up to the picture plane to get their true size. In the illustrations, you can see how this is done.

• Earlier, we briefly discussed the six basic types of technical drawing. Now we will look more closely at them.

Orthographic projection

• These are multi-view drawings showing, generally, three sides of an object. The front, top and side, of an object are projected so that they appear flat against the picture plane. In this way, each side can be seen clearly and measured. These are always drawn in a solid line. We use a dashed or hidden line to indicate what we can't see (such as a space or a hole inside an object,) The objects are dimensioned, which means their measurements or sizes are right on the drawings. A plan view is a single view showing only one side of the object.

• Once in a while, three sides cannot tell the whole story, so we need helper views. These auxiliaries are generally drawn when an object has an inclined or slanted surface. Because these angles are not at 90 degrees, we have to tip them up against the picture plane to measure and dimension them.

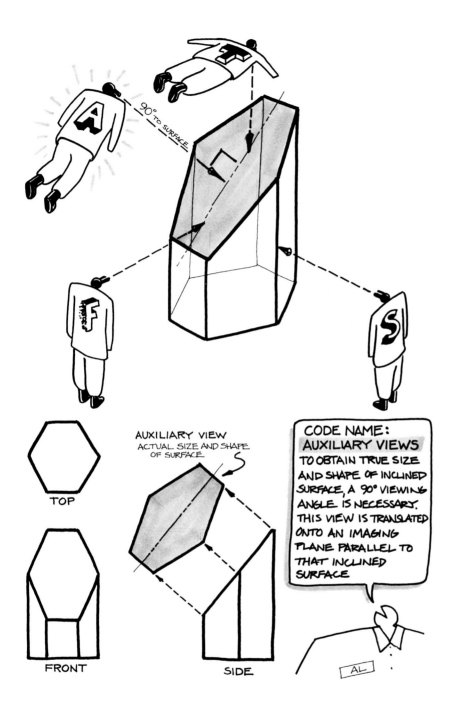

90° TO SURFACE

AUXILIARY VIEW
ACTUAL SIZE AND SHAPE
OF SURFACE

TOP

FRONT

SIDE

CODE NAME:
AUXILIARY VIEWS
TO OBTAIN TRUE SIZE
AND SHAPE OF INCLINED
SURFACE, A 90° VIEWING
ANGLE IS NECESSARY.
THIS VIEW IS TRANSLATED
ONTO AN IMAGING
PLANE PARALLEL TO
THAT INCLINED
SURFACE

AL

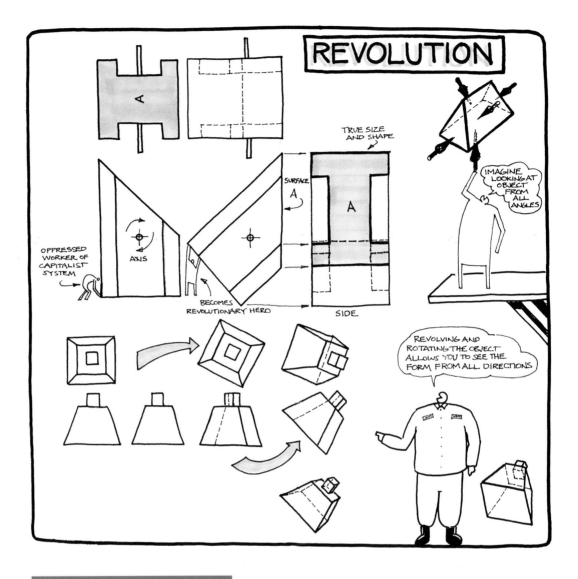

Revolutions

• Revolutions or rotations are also helper views. They are simply drawings of objects turned around as if on a center axis so that we can see all their sides.

CUTTING PLANE

TOP

BRRRRRRRRR

SECTION

CHILL OUT

CHILL OUT
THE EGGHEADS
YOLKS ON YOU RECORDS

Sections

• Showing all the parts of an object is often impossible, particularly if a lot of the parts are inside. In order to see in, we could use orthographic projection with hidden (dotted) lines, but it might become confusing. Instead, we can "slice it open" and look inside. In fact, we call the edge where the slice is made the cutting plane. Sections are useful in assembly drawings where you want to show how something with a number of parts is put together. Architects use sections to "see" inside a building.

Development and transition drawings

• If you unfold a cereal box and flatten it, you have a good example of a development drawing. In order to make containers from one sheet of material, a pattern must be made that has the outline and the fold lines. A development is simply a drawing of flat material, cardboard, sheet metal, plastic, that can be formed into a three-dimensional object.

• A transition is a specialized type of development drawing. Transition pieces are used in metal applications like duct work and piping where a single piece of material must have one square end and one round end. These pieces can get pretty complicated.

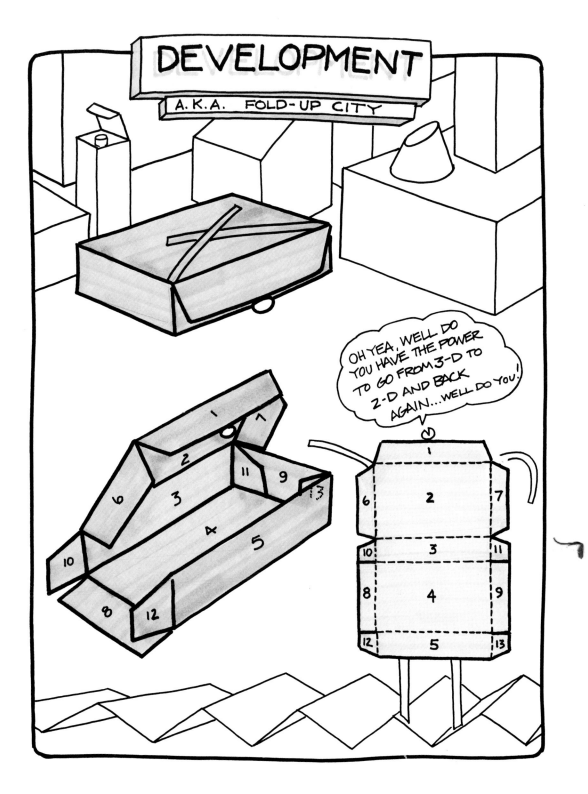

Pictorial drawings

- There are three basic type of pictorials: isometric, oblique and perspective views. All have one this in common: they attempt to show more than one side of an object in one view.

- An *isometric* drawing starts with the front edge of the object drawn against the picture plane and then goes back using parallel lines at an angle of 30 degrees. This way you can see three sides at once. A type of isometric drawing, called axonometric, might use other angles to reveal more of one side of an object. Architects use these quite a bit.

- *Oblique* drawings feature one side against the picture plane and one or more of the other sides going back. This way one side can be measured and examined but the illusion of depth is still there. Oblique drawings are sometimes called cabinet views because furniture makers traditionally draw their pieces this way.

- *Perspective* drawings are the most realistic. The object appears to recede into space in a normal way. The lines are not parallel. They converge the way railroad tracks do in the distance or a series of light poles do down a long, straight street.

Making choices

- A technical drawing communicates the specifics of a design from the creator to the makers. The designer who drafts must make a series of choices:

- What type or types of technical drawings am I going to use to convey the whole story about my design to others?

- How can I be most clear and most efficient?

- What must I do to make these drawings precise and accurate?

The wonderful thing about this type of communication is that everyone sees the same information. The designer can now get feedback about whether or not the object can be built, made, manufactured and/or constructed the way it was imagined.

- Sometimes you might develop a concept that looks beautiful on paper. But when you show it to those who have to make it, a sad truth is revealed. It just can't be done your way. Then you have to go back and actually revise your design. Maybe it can't be built for the right price or with a given material or in a certain amount of time. You can learn that type of information only when all participants in the design process are speaking the same language. The common language is technical drawing and that's why you have to know it.

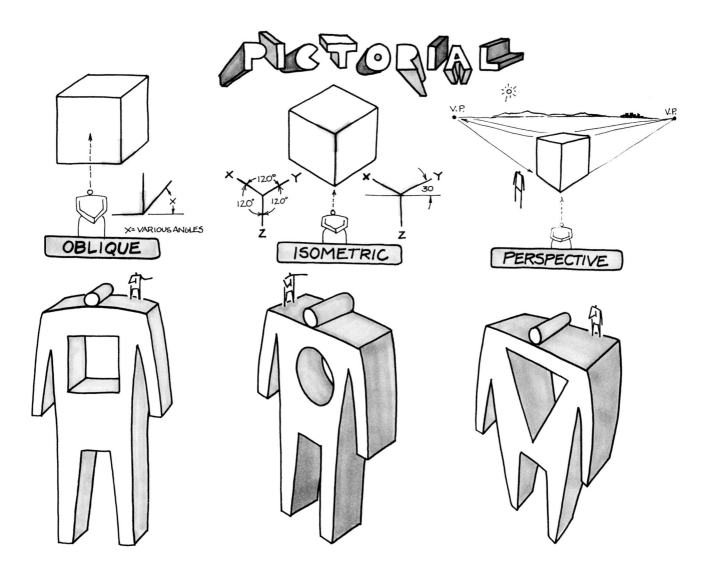

PICTORIAL

OBLIQUE

X= VARIOUS ANGLES

ISOMETRIC

120° 120° 120° 30°

PERSPECTIVE

V.P. V.P.

PACKAGING

It's been said that packaging is the 'kamikaze' of design. Why? The Japanese pilots in WW II willingly gave up their lives for a greater cause, and so does packaging. After the sale is made, the container, wrapping, and covering that protected the goods is sent to the deep. But what if packaging itself became an object of use? For instance, if you purchase a parakeet, how do you get it home? And when you do, where will it live? Wouldn't it be terrific if pet stores sold bird enclosures that could protect the creature in transit and then shelter the bird in your home?

Research packaging materials and the methods used to construct or fabricate a bird habitat. Your design should echo the appearance of your own house or apartment, so that the design becomes a miniature image of your own habitat. Naturally, your design should use a minimum of parts so that little assembly is needed. Keep in mind that parakeets are social creatures, quite colorful and alert, but they need to be covered at night in order to sleep.

One good reference point is food packaging. Your local supermarket is full of boxes for cookies, cereal, and spaghetti that are made from one piece of cardboard and then folded and glued together. Your bird habitat might be more complex, but you can use a similar design. Remember that such designs are laid out flat, so you'll have to make a development drawing. And don't forget the surface graphics. People are often swayed into purchasing one brand of product over another simply because the packaging is powerful and dynamic.

Philip Johnson
(American, 1906-)

Glass and steel: the ultimate in clean design. (Wiley House, Philip Johnson, Architect)

Johnson came to the study of architecture later in life, first serving as a curator at the Museum of Modern Art in New York City. In 1949, he designed his own house in the Miesian mode, in New Canaan, Conn. It was essentially a spare glass rectangle designed to bring the outside into the living space. His larger works include the Munson-Williams-Proctor Institute in Utica, New York, and the New York State Theater at Lincoln Center in New York City. These buildings further demonstrate his interest in the International style. Later, however, he reversed himself and in an abrupt return to historical architecture, designed the AT&T building in New York City, one of the first examples of Post-Modernism. This revivalist style features pared-down classical details, such as columns, arches and triangular pediments.

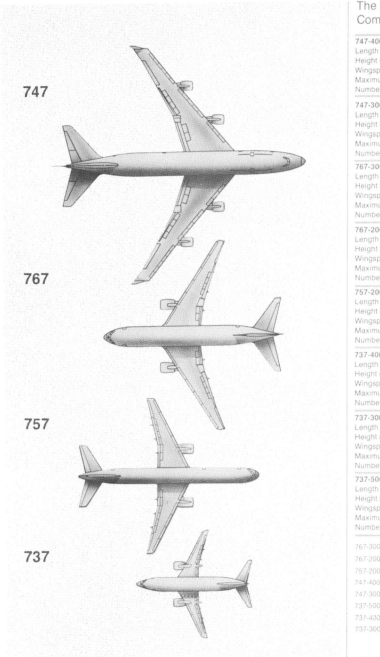

The First Family of Commercial Jet Airplanes

747-400
Length	231 ft 10 in.
Height (at tail)	63 ft 4 in.
Wingspan	211 ft
Maximum Gross Weight	870,000 lb
Number of Passengers	400

747-300
Length	231 ft 10 in.
Height (at tail)	63 ft 4 in.
Wingspan	195 ft 8 in.
Maximum Gross Weight	833,000 lb
Number of Passengers	400

767-300
Length	180 ft 3 in.
Height (at tail)	52 ft
Wingspan	156 ft 1 in.
Maximum Gross Weight	407,000 lb
Number of Passengers	210

767-200
Length	159 ft 2 in.
Height (at tail)	52 ft
Wingspan	156 ft 1 in.
Maximum Gross Weight	380,000 lb
Number of Passengers	174

757-200
Length	155 ft 3 in.
Height (at tail)	44 ft 6 in.
Wingspan	124 ft 10 in.
Maximum Gross Weight	220,000 lb
Number of Passengers	186

737-400
Length	119 ft 7 in.
Height (at tail)	36 ft 6 in.
Wingspan	94 ft 9 in.
Maximum Gross Weight	138,500 fb
Number of Passengers	146

737-300
Length	109 ft 7 in
Height (at tail)	36 ft 6 in.
Wingspan	94 ft 9 in.
Maximum Gross Weight	124,500 lb
Number of Passengers	128

737-500
Length	101 ft 9 in.
Height (at tail)	36 ft 6 in.
Wingspan	94 ft 9 in.
Maximum Gross Weight	115,500 lb
Number of Passengers	108

Range in Nautical Miles (bar chart: 767-300, 767-200, 757-200, 747-400, 747-300, 737-500, 737-400, 737-300; scale 0, 2,000, 4,000, 6,000, 8,000)

Boeing has one of the most successful design and production records in commercial aviation history. (Courtesy of Boeing)

The DESIGN AND production process is an organizational system.

It helps the people involved in the creative process to link up with the people responsible for the production process. This allows them to develop the best built, most exciting, attractively priced, and environmentally reputable product possible.

THE 11 STEPS OF DESIGN AND PRODUCTION

• In order minimize the cost of bringing a product to market and to maximize sales, an "economy of means" is necessary in design. In other words, doing the most with the least. To make the design process as efficient as possible, design professionals follow a series of steps. These steps increase the possibility that the client, the designer, the manufacturer and the public will all benefit from the product.

• Bringing a product to market often depends on good timing. Because they follow the same basic steps, the client and the industrial engineers can estimate the time needed for each part of the job. And the product out the door in a timely manner. Architectural and graphic

Good design is good business.
— *Thomas J. Watson, IBM*

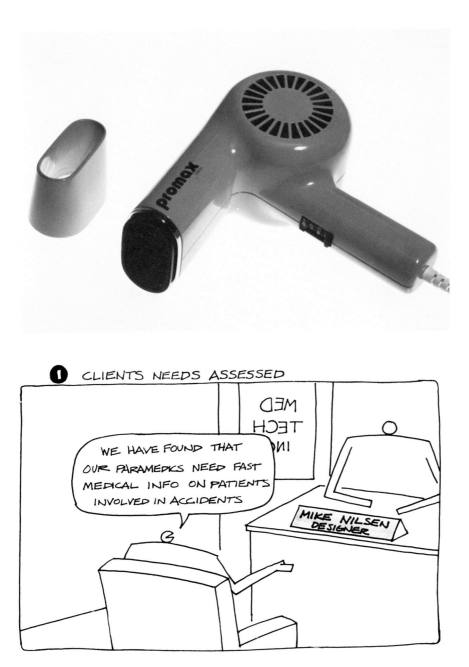

This simple but elegant form exemplifies a product that has gone through the entire design/production process. (Courtesy of Gillette)

design projects follow a similar procedure with adjustments depending on the specific design problem.

• Here are the eleven sequential steps in the design/production process:

1. The clients needs are assessed

• We start with an individual or an organization—a client who needs something designed. These people, the client, must decide whether or not it is feasible to build this new product. Designers can help with this decision.

• For instance, when Gillette got into the hairdryer business, their research showed that people were willing to spend up to twenty dollars for a multi-functional unit. They did more research and found out that young teenagers were interested in a lower cost model for about twelve dollars, one that didn't have a lot of features but was small and powerful.

• A team of designers was brought in to develop both models. The higher priced one was very sculptural, with highly textured parts including very smooth feeling switches. The lower cost dryer was bright yellow, with no decals. It was basically just two intersecting cylinders and one on/off switch. Both sold well because they were well positioned in the marketplace. The client had assessed its needs and found two holes in the market. It then set out to fill them in a very specific way.

2. Design conceptualization

• This is the designer's stage of development, where anything can happen. Professionals are not hampered by a lot of requirements. They can fly off in radical ways, challenge accepted design limitations and get down. You know, brainstorming ! Later on in the process the client will specify stricter requirements.

3. Visualization

• The designer prepares a series of sketches, drawings, renderings or simple models to provide a visual reference for the design ideas.

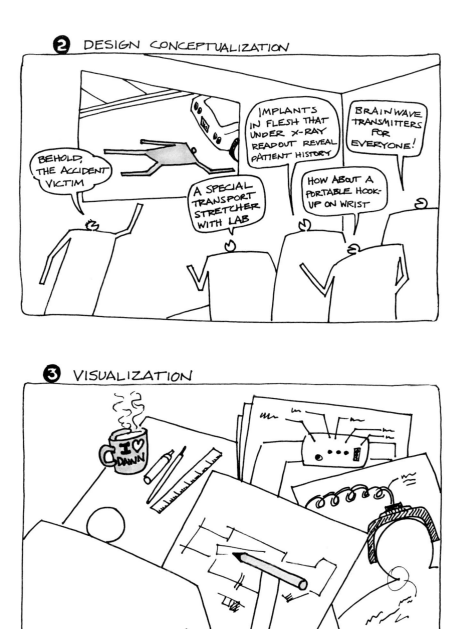

4. Presentation

• The design team meets with the client and presents their concepts. This meeting is often attended by marketing and production people, too. At this stage, environmental concerns might be aired.

5. Acceptance

• In the best case, the design is accepted and we move along toward the realization of the project. This, however, is rare. In the worst case, the designers are so far off they are dismissed. More frequently, the client decides or is told by the design team that what they want in a product is impossible at that price or in time to meet a deadline.

6. Redesign

• Back to step #3 for adjustments and revisions. Perhaps the design needs to be more exciting or more cost-effective. Perhaps the clients have decided they want something a bit more middle-of-the-road or they want a different part in a different color. From here, the process will continue to go back to step #3 and be repeated until all the bugs are worked out.

7. Working drawings

• The technical drawings, final models and support data are created and detailed. These are submitted to the manufacturing group.

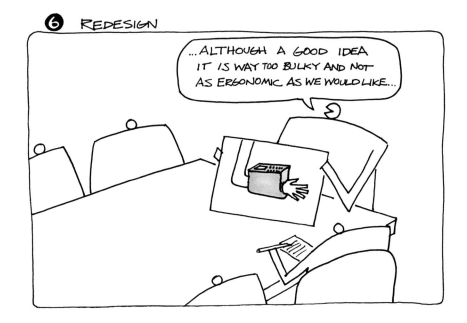

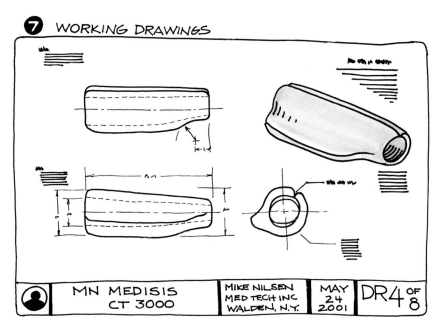

8. Marketing and sales

• While the final designs are being polished, the marketing/advertising pros develop their campaign to make potential buyers aware of the new product. Sales literature, packaging, spot commercials are all developed and tested. The advertising campaign is also a design process. The marketing/advertising people will use the same process the designers have used to satisfy the client's needs.

9. Prototypes are developed

• Samples are made by engineering. If necessary, they will recommend adjustments in either the design or manufacturing process.

10. Field testing

• Samples are taken "into the field." Potential customers handle them, use them, smell them, toss them around. Then they are quizzed on their responses to the product. Depending on how they respond, more adjustments might be made. Even at this late stage, a product might be postponed or even cancelled if the field test has been exceedingly negative. More often, it is full speed ahead.

11. Mass production

• Now it is time to make hundreds, thousands, or even millions of this product. It is time to place the piece in production. This is the world of **industry**: machinery, raw materials and manpower. Added to this are other major costs, such as shipping, advertising, and the disposal of waste.

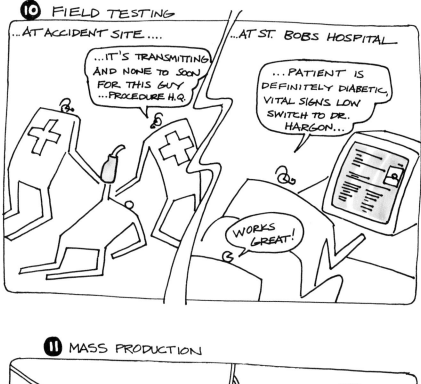

TECHNOLOGY AND MATERIALS

• A logical way to look at industry is to divide it into four technologies: manufacturing, construction, communications and transportation. The principal activity of industry is to convert raw materials into finished goods. But the process of conceiving, creating and developing a design is also an important part of all four technologies.

• In earlier chapters we learned how to communicate. But what happens to the idea and the drawing to turn a piece of paper or a model into the real thing? Since one objective of this book is to explore how to turn designs into objects, it is important to link the creative act and the drawing act to the production process.

• Simply put, production is either **manufacturing** or **construction**. When objects are made or assembled in a factory, we call the activity *manufacturing*. When the activity takes place on the site where the object is to be used, the process is called *construction*. A television is manufactured; a garage is constructed.

Manufacturing by hand on the old assembly line... And an artificial hand manufacturing on a new assembly line — a preferred method, particularly for the workers. (Courtesy of Henry Ford Museum and NASA)

Really, really old construction - but brilliant. After all, these are still with us... And, newer methods of building, which offer a greater range of styles because of available materials and processes. Will the structures we build be here long after us to define our times? (House photo courtesy of Davis A. Gaffga)

Paul Revere got the word out ahead of the British using an old method of communication. But, if the Redcoats had had new communication technology like this satellite dish, we'd be drinking much more tea and playing cricket. (Paul Revere photo courtesy of the Library of Congress)

- **Communications** is a part of industry we are familiar with. An important type of communication is graphic and, of course, you know by now that graphic communication is slick talk for communicating by drawing or imagemaking. But communications technology also refers to the graphic art of printing, telephones and fax machines—in fact, any way in which people get and give messages.

• And what about **transportation**? How else would a chair you designed get from the factory to the showroom, or the fabric to the factory, or the cotton from the fields to the mill? And how would the chair be moved about in the factory? People, too, are transported. Systems for getting you from the country to the city, up to the thirty-first floor or from Wichita to Hong Kong are a large part of our everyday world.

In the past, our possessions were limited by the method of transportation and the distance to be covered... It doesn't matter anymore. We are not limited in any way, except by the number of our closets and the depth of our wallets. (Courtesy of the Library of Congress and EDI Corp.)

FAMILY OF MATERIALS

GROUP	SUBGROUP	EXAMPLES
Metallics (metals and alloys)	*Ferrous*	Iron Steel Cast Iron Steel Alloys
	Nonferrous	Aluminum Tin Zinc Magnesium Copper Gold Nonferrous Alloys
	Powdered Metal	Sintered Steel Sintered Brass
Polymers	*Humanmade*	Plastics Elastomers Adhesives
	Natural	Rubber Bone Hide
Ceramics	*Crystalline Compounds*	Porcelain Structural Clay Abrasives
	Glass	Glassware Annealed Glass
Composites	*Wood-based*	Plywood Dimension Lumber Laminated Wood Impregnated Wood Paper
	Plastic-based	Fiber Glass Graphite Epoxy Plastic Laminates
	Metallic-based	Boron Aluminum Alumina Whiskers
	Concrete	Reinforced Concrete Asphalt Concrete
	Cermets	Tungsten Carbide Chromium Alumina
	Other	Reinforced Glass
Others	*Electronic*	Semiconductors
	Lubricants	Oil
	Fuels	Coal
	Protective	Anodized Coatings
	Biomaterials	Carbon Implants

MATERIALS AND THEIR PROPERTIES

• A good designer is familiar with may different types of materials. Some stuff can be bent and cut, but not rolled into smooth curves. Other materials are too soft to take heavy use or withstand changes in temperature. Some are cheap; others take color well. You've got to understand the properties, the characteristics, of materials so you can get the right material for your design idea.

• There are three basic types of materials used in production: metals, plastics (polymers) and ceramics. These materials can also be combined in various ways to create composite materials, which can take advantage of the better qualities of each element. A good example would be portland cement, sand and gravel. Alone, each material has very limited use in industry. Together they form concrete: a tremendously strong and enduring product that can be seen everywhere. (See the diagram for a list of metals, plastics, ceramics and composites.)

Metals

• Most metals are alloys. This means they are combinations of pure metals. The most widely used are iron-based, aluminum-based and copper-based alloys.

• Steel is an iron-based alloy. So is cast iron. The modern industrial world could not exist without iron for structural materials and orna-

mental shapes. Skyscrapers, automobiles, railbeds — none of these could exist without steel for strength and permanence. There are thousands of different grades of steel. Each grade has its own special characteristics that makes it right for a particular purpose.

• A designer does not have to know the qualities of all the steels, irons, and other metals used in industry. But you should understand strength, flexibility, durability and how the different metals look. There are different ways to form, cut, fasten and fabricate different metals, also. Although you won't have to weld joints or bolt plates together, a skilled designer must know how materials are fastened or connected to each other. Understanding these processes will affect your design conception.

Steel I-beams — our most basic engineered construction form — are the skeletons of our cities. (Courtesy of Bethlehem Steel)

Plastics

• Plastics, also called polymers, are manufactured materials. There are two different classes of plastic: thermoplastic and thermoset. *Thermoset* becomes permanent after being formed by heat and pressure. Once set, that's it. *Thermoplastic*, however, can be shaped and shaped again by repeating the forming process. It is easy to see how the two types could have different uses.

• Most plastics are made from a petroleum base reduced to a liquid or pellets. It is then sent to a manufacturer who blends various types of polymers together into a recipe. There are many, many ways to put plastics together. Each one features the special qualities determined by the product.

• Because polymer chains are so complex, they rarely biodegrade. As the awareness of our fragile ecology grows, polymer research is now geared toward producing useful plastics with environmentally responsible characteristics.

Shaped and formed, plastic can be elegant and refined. This German-designed steam iron could easily be sculpture. (Photo courtesy of Philippe Garner)

Ceramics

• Ceramic materials are naturally occurring. They are found in the earth in a raw state. Just like metals, ceramic must be refined and modified to be useful. Once formed, however, they are among the hardest of all materials.

Ceramics are replacing metals and plastics in many applications, from roof tiles to the tiles on the skin of the space shuttle.

• There are four groups of ceramics: clay-based ceramics, refractories, glass and cement.

• Clay is the stuff from which tiles, dinnerware, bathroom fixtures and false teeth are made. The amount of silica, or natural glass particles, in the clay determines how hard it will be. Clay is baked in ovens or furnaces into its final state. Different clay bodies need different amounts of heat to mature them (bake them until

Hot potato? Not really. Fresh from a 2300 F oven, this silicon cube can be held in bare hands. Ceramic material has the unique ability to take on and then cast off extremely hot temperatures. This is the stuff used for the space shuttle tiles. (Courtesy of NASA)

they are done). Earthenware, the crudest clay type, requires the lowest heat. China and porcelain are the finest types of clay and are used the most in industrial applications. Since they have a higher percentage of silica, they need higher temperatures to mature.

• A refractory is a clay with no silica. It is bonded at extremely high temperatures. Because it can take very high temperatures, it is used to line furnaces and cover the skin of the space shuttle. Refractory ceramics are also very lightweight.

• Glass is almost pure silica. Mineral content gives it color. If you extract all minerals, you'll get clear glass. You can control the color by adding just the right minerals. Although glass can be structural when made into blocks and bricks, it is the ability to transmit light and color that make it valuable as a decorative material.

Composites

• Lastly, composites are materials held or bonded together to take advantage of the special characteristics of each component. We think of wood as simply a natural material, but it is actually a natural composite. Hollow cellulose fibers in the wood are held together by lignin, a natural glue. Wood comes in different grades of hardness and softness and a magnificent array of colors and grains. Plywood is a composite manufactured from natural wood. Fiberglass and carbon fiber are other examples of composites.

Plywood and fiberglass — two composite materials. Each has special qualities that designers factor into a solution.

This is no place for a fashion experiment. Hostile environments challenge designers from all fields. (Courtesy of NASA)

surface texture, richness, elegance, rarity. But as you progress with the design, such lowly elements as cost and manufacturing can shatter your dream world. Sure, you can make a million-dollar tricycle out of gold studded with diamonds, but will anybody buy it?

Know your material

• Good designers, however, can turn manufacturing restrictions into advantages, particularly if they know material properties. Maybe your design calls for a product with strength, durability, weight, flexibility and toughness. These properties can be found in many different materials. Does the material need to stand up to extremes of hot or cold? Does it have to go from one to the other without damage? Then you should understand thermal properties. Some products call for very dense materials; others require porosity. Some products must be used in corrosive environments. Some have to conduct or resist electricity and magnetism. Optical properties — the ability of a material to block, absorb or transmit light — are desirable for some designs. Transmitting or absorbing sound can be important, too.

• Designers always struggle with materials. Often it's a battleground, with the creatives on one side and the engineers on the other. Generally they reach a solution by compromising between cost, manufacturing and aesthetic

The million-dollar tricycle

• When designers are in the planning stages, they imagine the finished object and the material from which it will be made. They are looking for the materials with just the right properties to interpret their ideas. It is critical that designers feel free to explore an idea without restrictions that limit their style. And in this age, almost anything that can be imagined can be made. Therefore, your first consideration might be purely aesthetic. You might choose a material for such properties as warmth, color,

issues. Incidentally, this is one of the differences between fine art. In fine art you rarely have to compromise your ideas for the sake of the group effort. In design, everyone shares responsibility for the success or failure of the project. And there is plenty of compromise.

A typical 'Gore-tex' application.

Sometimes you have to start from scratch

• Once in a rare while, someone solves a problem by creating not just the design, but the actual material. That's total control.

The story of Gore-Tex

• Bill Gore was such a person. An avid outdoorsman, he would become annoyed when rainstorms interrupted his commune with nature. He found that a yellow slicker and other nylon or cotton rain gear were good at keeping out the wet, but were uncomfortable because they kept in body heat and moisture from perspiration.

• So he set out to create a material, a fabric that could "breathe." Eventually he developed a thin, membrane-like cloth that let air reach the skin and wicked away perspiration and heat, but refuse to allow water to soak in. At first he couldn't make it pliable enough. Sandwiched between the outer and inner layers of a jacket, it made a crackling, crunching noise. Eventually, he refined the fabric into an unnoticed waterproofing system we now call "Gore-Tex."

• Single-handedly, Gore revived

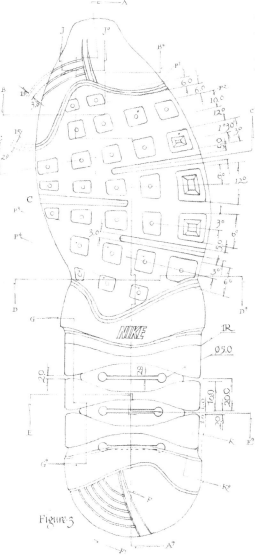

Figure 3

can be enhanced so that it can be used in new and different ways.

Putting shoes on the waffle iron

- The invention of the modern running shoe is a similar story. Bill Bowerman wanted to improve traction on cross-country running trails in Oregon. So he used a waffle iron to form a thermoplastic compound into a grid-like sole. And that was the beginning of the hugely successful Nike company.

- Nike spends an enormous amount of money in research and development, seeking new materials and applications of those materials. As a result, they make shoes that serve a particular need extraordinarily well. Shoe designers at Nike have great knowledge of material properties, the mechanics of the foot and the latest trends in fashion. At the present time, I can't think of any better example of the marriage of art and science.

COMMUNICATIONS TECHNOLOGY

- When we think of communications, the first things that comes to mind are the human voice, writing, and perhaps some type of signaling system. If we stop at that point, we will only have recognized the most basic, common

the entire outdoor clothing market. Since its invention corresponded with the fitness trend of the 1970s, his product was used in rain parkas, running and climbing gear, hats, gloves and in the latest form, shoes. It is a good example of how a single property of a material

RECYCLING CONTAINERS

The word is recycle. Everyone is doing it because we know that if we don't take measures now, we'll drown in our own waste. Today, when waste is removed from my street, I have to separate the paper products from clear glass, the plastic from newspapers and the household garbage from brown glass. In most communities, it now takes a least four containers to accommodate household waste. My garage is being overrun by trash containers. To further the problem you not only have to store it but you've got to get the stuff down to the curb. Apartment buildings and office towers are faced with the same problems on an immense scale. Trash haulers must pay by weight when they dump and are charged or fined when the garbage is not separated. Since this is a problem that will not go away, what can we do to make the process easier and more efficient?

Consider the following: we have to store stuff that is smelly, heavy, and bulky. When it is wet, trash can get very heavy indeed. All of the material must be transported from the house to the street once per week. So what can we design that will accomplish the task and be washable, weather resistant and sturdy? In some cases, people who live in apartments must take their waste to stations on their floor or down the elevator to a holding station. In suburbia, the larger volume means a longer trip.

The containers need to be easily filled, transported, and cleaned up. Their contents should be easily identifiable, and they should take a minimum of space and last a long time. Do not be limited by the term "container." The solution will be a major success simply because every household needs one.

There is no room for guesswork when it's your responsibility to tell a commercial aircraft when and where to land. It's communication between humans and machines that permits the airline industry to operate safely. (Courtesy of GM/Hughes)

information they tell and what type of reaction the human expresses all depend on the skill of the designer.

• Quite often an object tells us something and we must react. It might be a room thermostat, the buzzer on a smoke alarm, or a low fuel reading on the dashboard. If the information is clear and easily understood, then the design is effective.

The human/machine interface

• It is particularly important that designers be aware of the "interface" between humans and machines. As we discovered in earlier chapters, the point of visual and physical connection with an object puts the skills of the designer to the test.

• You know, the first point of physical contact between person and machine is often an on/off switch. This simple, inexpensive and sometimes overlooked item can tell a lot about a product. Better lamps, cars, even better motel rooms have higher quality switches. They feel solid and smooth; some are even silent. Compare other "insignificant" details, such as automobile door handles, coffee machines, computer keyboards. You'll see what I mean.

The power of communication

• From the earliest speech and alphabets, from the beginning of printing to the latest fax machines and cellular phones, technology

aspects of human communication. In fact, another important type of communication is human to machine and machines to human.

Communicating with machines

• Information to be understood from signs, the location and appearance of automobile gauges, the sound and feel of an electric razor, the smell of a leather jacket — these all communicate messages. How effectively those messages are understood, what kind of

Eero Saarinen
(Finnish-American, 1910-61)

Saarinen's family moved to the United States in 1923 and he followed his father, Eliel, into design. After he worked for the industrial designer Norman Bel Geddes, he designed furniture with Florence Knoll. His "Womb" chair and "Tulip" chair were elegant plastic and aluminum creations both modern and timeless. Organic shapes and experimental materials in product design led naturally to that same design sense in architecture. The TWA terminal at Kennedy Airport in New York, 1956-62 and the Kresge Auditorium at MIT in 1955. Both feature concrete as a sculptural, fluid exterior element. In that way, his work reminds us of the work of Le Corbusier.

Space voyagers of the 21st century would look good in this Saarinen pedestal chair. (Courtesy of Knoll International)

impossible to overestimate the importance of communications.

• The best designs are those that clearly express not only what they are, but a sense of quality and importance. In order for a designer to achieve that greatness, the design itself must not only "speak" to people but allow people to speak back to it. The design has to communicate. Any time you create something for human use, remember the human. After all, the design adjusts to us; the weaker design forces us to adjust to it.

New communication technologies

• So where does technology come into this? Well, only you can control the point of interface. A switch, a handle, a gauge, an instrument of measurement all must easily tell the user what its purpose is and what's going on. A person must be able to read the dial, turn the crank, throw the switch, or adjust the meter easily and precisely.

One-hundredth of a second from now...

• The silicon chip permits time to be broken down and measured in hundredths of a second, and then shown to us on a liquid crystal display. This technology allow us to manipulate time with great precision. When you edit videotape from two VCR's, you can match the end of one scene exactly to the beginning of the next. Instead

Beam me up, Scotty! The power to "reach out" exists in the form of a hand-held, pocketable, cellular phone. (Courtesy of Motorola)

has opened pathways to faster and faster communications. As new technologies become more common, designers must get better at improving the connection between us and machines. Messages are both intellectual and emotional. They inform, instruct, persuade or entertain. So the designer has to learn a bit about human psychology. Since a designer's job is to make products, graphics, buildings useful, enjoyable — even fascinating — it would be

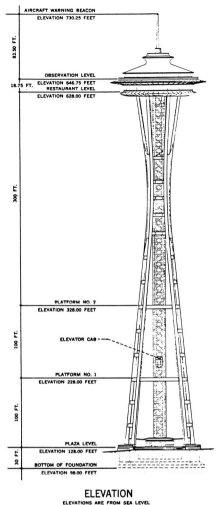

of rewinding by hand or using a stopwatch to time the exact moment, the readouts on each machine measure to the precise micro-second. The machines adjust themselves to the moment, and then one plays and the other records. This precision is not just a function of high technology; it is how the machine tells the person what's going on. The person can then guide the machine to do just the right amount of work. And it is not just pressing buttons, either. Because designers and engineers know that our fingers are precision tools, most editing-type VCR's have a large wheel that can be rotated quite a ways to move the tape even a little bit. Why? So we could easily adjust the machine in a very human way. That's effective communication.

• Perhaps the most human way to interact with the machine is to talk to it. The voice activated computer may soon be a reality. When that happens, you'll have a machine that will recognize your voice and follow your spoken commands. The keyboard, mouse, tablet or any other type of input device will become less important. The feel and touch of the keyboard might be replaced by the volume and strength of your words. Will that improve communications? Will it put an end to the written language?

• Stick around and we'll find out.

TRANSPORTATION

• Moving messages from people to people, machine to machine and machine to people is communications. Moving people and material from place to place is transportation. We have spoken briefly about designs for transportation: autos, trains, etc. It is

Ferries like this Seattle hydrofoil are fast, efficient alternatives to commuting by automobile. The Space Needle at left first existed in architect John Graham's mind and then as a drawing. (Drawing from Metropolis Magazine)

also important to understand the process of transportation itself—getting things from here to there.

How will it be shipped?

• Occasionally, transportation can determine the actual design of an object. For instance, changing the outside shape or dimensions or weight of a television might permit more to be shipped at one time, saving a few dollars on the cost of each unit. The final price of everything we buy includes the cost of transporting the goods from the place it was made, assembled or even grown, to the final point of sale, the place were someone buys it. The movement of the raw material to the factory and the cost of shipping materials to a building site are also included into the final price of anything offered for sale.

• Personal transportation means moving people and things ourselves. Driving to work, moving your own furniture, bringing lumber to your house from a home center, taking a family on vacation are examples of personal transportation. Commercial transportation is moving people for profit, using buses, trains and planes. Everything else that's moved is called cargo or freight.

• Cargo is moved along the highways, by rail, water and air. In fact, there are transport systems underground, too. Oil and gas, electricity and phone messages are moved along pipelines or cables. Many of these are underground.

From the factory to the store

• Transportation systems rely on each other to send freight from point to point. As an example, let's follow your newly designed portable phone from the factory to a store for test marketing. The one hundred units are picked up from the final assembly point by a straight body truck and delivered to a large warehouse on the edge of town. Here, it is loaded onto a semi-trailer as part of a much larger shipment of all kinds of different items. Off it goes to another city, perhaps hundreds of miles away, where it again is separated at another "break-bulk" warehouse. It is then placed on another, smaller truck or van and delivered to the store.

• The transportation system chosen is usually determined by the cost of the service, and that's measured by the weight of the cargo. Some shippers can only handle up to specific sizes. Sometimes things are needed in a hurry and you have to pay more for faster service. Other carriers offer better protection against breakage, better schedules, cheaper, if you ship at different times of the day or night, week or even month.

• There are certain types of cargo that require specialized vehicles, too. Hazardous materials, like chemicals and nuclear fuels, or unusually large objects like steel pipes. These are shipped over specific routes using specially designed trucks, barges or freight trains.

Trains carry freight more economically and with less environmental damage than any other form of transportation. The coal on this one will power electrical generating plants. (Courtesy of Southern Railway)

- How about moving large objects around in a factory or job site? This type of transportation is called materials handling. Conveyor belts, endless loops of rubber treads, move boxes around a plant. Overhead there might be hooks that carry car bodies into a paint bath and out again. Industrial cranes move heavy loads inside large factories. Small trucks like forklifts scoot around construction sites with materials too heavy or bulky for people to carry.
- People are sometimes freight, too. Elevators, escalators, moving sidewalks, monorails and tramways move us up, down, around — in office buildings, amusement parks or on the ski slopes.

WILL IT LOOK LIKE WHAT YOU IMAGINED?

- Throughout this chapter, we've linked the creative side of design to the real world of industry. Getting the building built, the product on the shelves, the ad in the magazine means using processes far removed from the simplicity of a person sketching on a pad in a studio. The more you understand the entire process, from design conception to product realization, the better the chances are that what you imagine will actually be made. The designer does not have the freedom artists have to just please themselves.
- Designers rarely touch the finished product. Instead they must transfer the idea for a solution from head to hand in drawings and models. The architect doesn't actually build the building; the product designer doesn't construct the stereo; the graphic designer doesn't print the new logotype. And that's what makes the task so special and so difficult. No matter how good a designer you are, you always have to guess what the finished thing will look like.
- If you are really good, the idea, energy and emotional qualities will carry over from your head and heart. Then everyone else involved in building the skyscraper, fabricating the stereo or printing the new logo will be just as excited as you. If the user, the client, also gets the same sensation and excitement, you will be hailed as a truly great artist.

NEW FLAG

What is a flag? A nation's identity. A symbol of meaning for a people. An emblem that says "I believe in all the great things for which this country stands?" A bunch of colors on a piece of cloth or paper? A graphic design? A cause for anger, hatred, exclusion? A passion, a longing?

Like all designs that are essentially abstract, we give our flag it's meaning. You know other nations' people feel the same way about their own colors and their own abstract images. There are good reasons for the designs to be abstract also: they are easy to reproduce and visible from a long distance. They also lend themselves to bright coloration. Our flag represents history — the stars are the fifty states, the stripes the original thirteen colonies. What would happen if we decided to celebrate other events in our history and design our flag around those elements?

Suppose we wanted to celebrate the USA as a place of "spacious skies, amber waves of grain and purple mountains majesty." What would the flag look like then? Or if we wanted to focus on the fact that our nation is made up of all sorts of immigrants who came to the country at different times. How might we represent that image? Or if we wanted to celebrate the U.S. cities?

You have the opportunity to design a new flag for the United States of America. What should it look like? Let's not look only to history for reference but to the present as well. Maybe our new flag will look similar to the "stars and stripes." Maybe not. Use the same proportions for the shape, but choose any images or colors. Naturally, you will have a clear reason for each part of your flag since the flag is an emotional and powerful object.

Yes, success is often measured by the solution to an important problem. The Eiffel Tower (1889) was, and still is, a success. The Tacoma Narrows Bridge, which self-destructed during a storm in 1940, was not. (Courtesy of George Barford and University of Washington Libraries)

It's time
for you,

THE BEGINNING DESIGNER,

to confront
your ability

to successfully complete an assignment. All along, you have made decisions about many things: color, shape, texture, materials, size, weight, graphics, symbols, images, emotional qualities, drawing methods, art tools, renderings, models and so on, and so on, etc, etc, etc. When a person gets involved in making so many decisions, a lot of personal energy becomes invested in the solution. Sometimes — no, usually — t is difficult to be objective about the success or failure of a particular design.

• Throughout the long development process many people will examine your work: teachers and fellow students, colleagues, your boss and, in some cases, the clients. Perhaps suggestions are made. Some you act on, making suitable adjustments. On other issues, you learn to trust your own personal vision and hold firm against changes.

• Formative, or in-progress, evaluation is useful because it allows you to see your efforts through other eyes. You may think that you're answering the problem in one way, but find out that it's being received another way. It is as if you were speaking perfectly correct English to people who speak nothing but French. You know what message you are sending, but they are not getting it.

THE CRITIQUE

• In the advertising business, there comes a time when the creative team has to pitch, or sell, their ideas to management before meeting the client. A typical case

Discussion and defense often lead to better solutions.

A typical student assignment with specific criteria to be achieved.

is during a logo or corporate image assignment. The artists hang their rough sketches on a corkboard wall for everyone to see. The staffs looks over the sketches and then offers their criticism. Usually during this "critique," as it is called, a design or a few designs will spark the imagination of someone to go further, to answer the problem even more effectively. Because this process takes place before the final solution, before the forming of the finished answer, it is part of the formative evaluation.

Student evaluation

• A student is often asked to show work in progress before the class. It's the same basic process. There is a problem to solve. Let's see how you are doing.

• It is vitally important to display all your beginning ideas and preliminary sketches. For (just as in the example of the advertising critique) you might have hit on a

goody and not recognize it. A classmate could identify some particularly clever design that you dismissed as unimportant. A teacher might discover a piece of potential brilliance, while to your untrained eye, it was just a bunch of scribbles.

• A fair question for you to ask at this point is, what are they looking for? Well, it is really simple: Did you meet all the criteria? And are you getting the right message across.

Did you meet all the criteria?

• Firstly, the teacher, the boss, the client, are looking for an answer to the original problem. Did you satisfy the basic requirements concerning size, weight, color, market appeal, price, etc. Can five people live in the house you designed. Or can the logo you designed be recognized on stationery, on a shirt or on the side of a truck? Those are objective criteria. You can measure your solution against a clear set of requirements.

What is the message?

• Secondly, what are the subjective messages your project is communicating? These are not as clear or as easy to judge, but quite significant. Does the portable hand mixer look exciting and sleek? How is it different within the competitive environment? Is the automobile sleek and expensive looking? Does the book cover look mysterious and intriguing? And the ever popular: is it beautiful?

Hard and soft evaluation

• Let's go back to our discussion about metaphors. You might recall we talked about "hard" and "soft" thinking. Hard referred to logic, reason, precision; soft was about emotion, play, approximation. Those distinctions can apply to evaluation. The criteria (fixed, specific and measurable) are hard; the subjective concerns (personal, indefinite and emotional) are soft. On some projects, the client will insist on one set over the other. The greatest designs, however, are those solutions that fulfill all the expectations of the criteria and still integrate emotional content to give meaning, importance and excitement. Then society gets a building, wristwatch or corporate symbol with style, power, grace and beauty.

• In our culture we have always admired objects that are "classics." These are designs that endure over time because they make some sort of statement that we can relate to emotionally.

The Chrysler Building (William Van Alen, 1928-30) versus the Empire State Building (Shreve, Lamb and Harmon, 1929-31). Which has more power to be remembered as a structure with style and grace? Which looks like a giant stepped pyramid? (Courtesy of the NYC Visitor's Bureau)

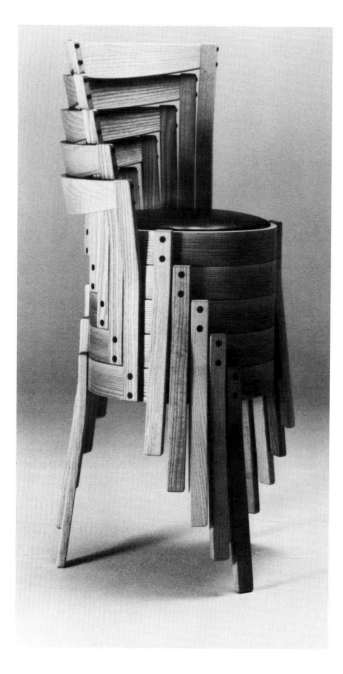

• Compare two skyscrapers: the Chrysler Building and the Empire State Building. Both were built for the same purpose and within a few years of each other. They both answer the same problem. But one has endured as the very symbol of the drama and excitement of metropolitan life. The other is remembered as a real tall building. Why? Take a look and see if you can tell.

Talking up your design

• This is a good time for you to understand the value of public speaking. Maybe this topic seems a bit far out. Actually, it is a skill every designer must develop. You will have to express yourself clearly in "design talk." Often, you will have to verbally defend your work. Someone is bound to ask "why." Why did you choose this color or that material? Why is that shape used for a handle? What was your thinking on the form of that chair? What made you associate that object with speed, or excitement or a modernist style? Your answers should include a clear statement of what you intended, why you chose that particular solution and why you think it it answers the problem. You also want to express any special quality or benefits from your solution.

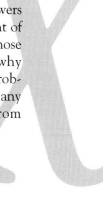

A great solution to a mundane problem — stackability. A very neat and crisp design. Nice texture in the wood grain, too. (Courtesy of Curtis Erpelding, designer)

WORKING AS A TEAM

• Often, you'll be working as part of a team. In a small creative group, each individual assumes a role. One person might be the crazy, innovative one, while someone else is the detail person, asking difficult technical questions. You might be the one to present the final design to a review panel.

• To get along on a team, you have to be forceful about your own beliefs, but willing to listen hard to others who feel just as strongly. You must learn to walk the fine line between defending your personal vision and giving in to a homogenized solution that makes everyone a little happy. It is said that a camel is a horse designed by a committee. Strive to work within the team, but never fail to press your beliefs. When compromise and conviction are in conflict, go with your conviction.

MEANWHILE, OUT IN THE REAL WORLD

• Because design is art done for others, conflict can arise between clients and designers. To a client, selecting a free-lance designer or hiring a designer to work on staff is a complex decision. Can the designer do the job, fit in with the existing staff, respond well to deadlines and pressures? Can we have a good relationship, over time?

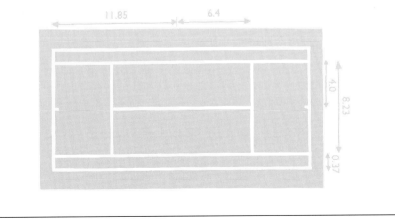

DESIGN
Challenge

SPORTS

As we enter the twenty-first century, we recognize more similarities among the peoples of the earth. One strong identifier of any culture is the sports that people play. Throughout this century we have tried to spread American games across the oceans. Baseball is popular in Japan, and football has caught on in Europe. Soccer keeps gaining popularity here as newer Americans continue to keep it as their primary sport. Interestingly, as sports games go into new places, the rules, the equipment, the training routines, uniforms and stadiums change. Professional sports are constantly being monitored for change because they are big money enterprises. Every modification is carefully thought out — not only to make the game easier to understand, but to heighten the action and excitement.

Choose a sport and write a brief paragraph expressing your thoughts on how that sport will change over the next ten years. Think about rules, equipment, uniforms, playing fields, tracks and anything else that you think could or should happen to make the game more understandable or more thrilling.

Once you complete the writing you will illustrate your own ideas for changes. This should be done with a drawing and a caption explaining each change so that any person can pick up your work and grasp your ideas.

(Courtesy of Gerald Brommer)

• The designer often wonders: Will they let me be creative and express my wild ideas? Is the work environment challenging but not impossible? Does this company think design is as important as other aspects of its business?

YOUR PORTFOLIO

• The dictionary defines a portfolio as, "A flat, portable case for carrying loose papers, drawings, etc." Well that's technically what a portfolio is, but it is also a lot more than that, too.

• A portfolio is a visual portrait of you. It's a platform from which you speak your beliefs, your answers, your talents, your efforts, your energy. Without a portfolio, your ideas and innovations would never be seen. You'd never have the opportunity to share and improve yourself. The portfolio is a point of departure where you can sail out your work to cause discussion and interest.

• The portfolio used to be thought of as a summative instrument (and still is in some places). This means it is the place to show only your best stuff, your finished pieces, the ones that demonstrate your genius. More often though, particularly in a school situation, a portfolio also shows off your thinking, your process.

• It is important to demonstrate how you attacked a problem, the stages of development the design went through before it was completed. A body of work that

(Courtesy of Charrette)

demonstrates changes over time is truly the best way to measure your progress and success. You can reflect on what you did in the past and the critical decisions you made. This will not only enhance your portfolio, it will also be valuable when you tackle new assignments.

What should you put in your portfolio?

• Keep in mind that a portfolio is situational. This means that you constantly adjust it by adding or subtracting pieces depending on the audience. Teachers will want to see your developmental work as well as your finished work. A potential employer might like a few conceptual "idea" pieces, but really wants to see completed projects.

The process portfolio

• If we look at the portfolio as a formative tool, it should include raw sketches — thumbnails, trash paper roughs, doodles scrawled on napkins, anything you use to express a part of the answer.

• Sometimes, it is useful to include other types of information. You might put in the historical research you did, any special readings that helped on a problem, xerox copies of articles from journals or magazines, pictures of interesting shapes and forms, textures that influenced you. Maybe some artworks inspired your solution, even if they have little direct meaning. Poetry about a time or place, music that set a mood— anything that contributed toward the solution. Not only are these elements important in your portfolio, but they will help during a defense of your work, when you present ideas to your creative team, teacher or client.

• This type of portfolio is often called a "process folio," because it shows the steps you took to merge a lot of unattached information into the final piece. The things you choose to put in the portfolio gives others a clue about what size mind you have and how you turn vague ideas into concrete reality.

The summative portfolio

• A summative portfolio, one you might use to get a job, is a bit different.
• How different?
• It is difficult to say. Employers, or colleges you might apply to, have varying requirements. A general rule of thumb would be to compile your best finished pieces, supported by some preliminary material that demonstrates your problem-solving abilities.
• Naturally, a portfolio for an aspiring architect would feature projects of varying types of buildings. These would show the range of your experience. In addition to freehand drawings and sketches, there should be technical solutions — working drawings, blueprints, CAD work. Photographic slides of completed projects and models are valuable, too.

• An industrial designer's portfolio would look similar to an architects, although there might be a greater opportunity to show some work that can be held or used.
• A graphic designer's portfolio would rely more on conceptual drawings, roughs and idea pieces, supported by printed examples of completed designs in a variety of applications.

Your silent representative

• All portfolios should show off graphic skills. Pieces should be varied also by technique: color renderings, precise drawings, a wide range of art tools. They should be clean and well presented. Loose drawings should be permanently mounted. They must be clean and kept that way. The actual case should be easy to open and close. Make sure it is easy to get the pieces in and out to save embarrassment. It must be easy for others to gain access to everything.
• The portfolio is a demonstration of your thinking, problem-solving and drawing skills. Because a portfolio is often examined when you're not around, it's your silent representative left behind to make an impression. To sell you to people from whom you want something — that is the major job of the portfolio.

Florence Knoll

(American, 1917-)

Knoll trained as a furniture designer at the Cranbrook Institute and with Mies van der Rohe at the Illinois Institute of Technology. With her husband, Hans, she set up Knoll Associates and produced furniture for corporate interiors. Although she created quite a few pieces of her own, she also revived Bauhaus pieces and collaborated with Eero Saarinen and others. The interiors have clean lines and edges, rich textured materials and totally integrated work spaces. Knoll Associates' work can be seen at CBS headquarters in New York, and the Connecticut General Life Insurance Company, Hartford, Connecticut.

Classic geometric shapes of these Knoll designs echo the principles of Walter Gropius and the Bauhaus. (Courtesy of Knoll International)

How many brands of detergent do we really need? What would happen if there were only one brand? (Photo by Wyatt Wade)

EPILOGUE

I'd love to describe design as **AN ACTIVITY OF THE PUREST TYPE AND** a most noble pursuit.

But that would be less than accurate. There are people who might actually make a case against design and even against a book such as this.

DO WE NEED ALL THIS STUFF?

• Since design functions as a tool for selling, it goes a long way toward fueling commercial interests. Just look at the incredible amount of junk toys we manufacture for children. In the supermarket you're bombarded by hundreds of products that are virtually identical. Millions of trees are cut down just for the packaging alone.

• "Why do we need more things?" could be a fair rallying cry. We are, after all, a wasteful consumer society. We use things up and toss them away. We make more and more stuff and then can't understand why mountains of garbage accumulate at our landfills and dumps. By the turn of the century, the Fresh Kills dump on Staten Island will share an unusual honor with the Great Wall of China: the Fresh Kills dump and the Great Wall will be the only two human-made objects identifiable from space.

Few human designs compare in scale to the Great Wall of China, which stretches for almost 2500 miles.

• And worst of all, we are addicted to Mr. Hydrocarbon. Oil is the fuel for our cars and the source of our plastic. Synthetic fabrics, construction products, wall coverings, floor coverings and paint are all by-products of the petroleum industry. Oil causes fortunes to rise and fall. Wars are fought over it. It pollutes our air and our water supply. Ultimately it will poison our planet. And every day, our supplies of this poisonous, deadly, desperately needed fuel keep shrinking and shrinking.

The designer's role

• In an age of diminishing resources, fouled environment and ridiculous overabundance, overproduction and overselling of products, can designers really have any influence? How can we satisfy humanity's desire for useful, glorious objects and not destroy our fragile globe? Must we sacrifice a bit of the ozone layer for each new stereo?

• I think not.

• Design answers society's need for useful objects, constructs and information. Design changes as human needs change. As individuals, families, communities, cities and nations refashion and evolve, the objects — the tools, vehicles and toasters — change, too.

An economy of means

• But designers must also work within an "economy of means." Although I mentioned this before,

• We use up natural resources at an alarming rate with no regard for the future. We tear up forests, carve into the earth and pour toxic gases into the atmosphere. Manufacturing and refining processes, while turning raw materials into useful products, often create hazardous, lethal by-products. And we can't figure out how to dispose of those, either.

• The danger doesn't end when the product is installed. Many new products, such as carpeting and furniture, give off toxic vapors. This is a serious problem in modern office buildings where the climate is controlled by remote sensors and windows do not open. Chemical treatments for stain resistance and fireproofing also circulate through air exchangers and not enough fresh air is introduced. So people are getting sick at work.

Acid rain may be killing large tracts of forests, both in the Eastern U.S. and parts of Europe. It's the pollutants from burning oil and other hydrocarbon fuels such as coal that cause the rain to turn sour. Designers must consider such impacts in their attempts to solve technological problems. (Courtesy of the USDA Forest Service)

perhaps now you can see its true importance. For an "economy of means" refers to a design solution that uses as little material as possible, as effectively as possible, with a minimum of cost, labor and impact on the environment. As we become, hopefully, more energy conscious and environmentally aware, a conservation factor will become part of the design criteria.

The consumer/designer connection

• Design is a human experience; people can influence design. If we as individual consumers insist on environmentally conscious designs, manufacturers must take heed. This is because design is market-driven; designs are created when the need exists, not just for their own sake. If consumers buy only what's environmentally credible, designers will have to respond. Industrial/commercial standards will have to change.

• Designers will then have a professional responsibility to create products, buildings and images that, at the very best, enhance our environment and at the very least, do a minimum of harm. In this way, we designers can become leaders in creating a balance between need and responsibility.

Quality = profit

• Quality is the most important issue facing companies today besides, in my opinion, environmental considerations. Constant improvement in manufacturing processes and product reliability can insure profits for the company. But if quality is to be the real focus, then more firms must learn, or relearn, how to design and market. Anticipating the needs of the customer is certainly an important part of industry. But sometimes, a product is of such high quality, or the idea is so strong, that the need follows in the wake of the product. No consumer asked for the discovery of electricity, the camera, the copying machine or the "post-it" note. But how could we do without them today?

COPING WITH BRAVE NEW TECHNOLOGY

• At the turn of the last century, most people lived on farms and grew or raised everything they needed. Automobiles were a tinkerer's dream and soaring to the moon was the stuff of science fiction. During this century, we've become comfortable with an mind-blowing array of devices.

• Think of how people have had to adjust, learn new skills, talk a new language. We talk easily about Nintendo, ATMs, faxes, xeroxes, cellular phones. We cook in a device that stimulates electrons in food (a microwave oven) and move about in metallic containers, assisted by electronic brains, that propel us at 60 miles an hour. Our wristwatches bleep out our appointments, record our heart rate, dial our phones, and come with 64-page instruction manuals.

• We are surrounded by many complex devices at home, at school, at work, even at play. Technology is outstripping our ability to comprehend and operate it. Some people are intimidated by it all, drop out and refuse to cooperate. The rest of us at one time were comfortable with, even excited by, all these things. But now we are being overwhelmed by the sheer number of products in our lives.

• I've just installed a new telephone in my office and I'm frustrated because I can't master all the technologic power to do great, timesaving tasks. I get an anxiety attack when the power goes out in my neighborhood. I have to reset ten clocks, not to mention radio pre-sets, the VCR taping schedule and the computerized thermostat. Then there's the time change from daylight savings to standard time. *Holy cow, here we go again.*

A technology overload

• I'm suggesting there is a growing number of folks who are not among the technologically impaired or illiterate, but who are becoming overwhelmed by the amount of technology and its complexity. They cannot use the technology to its fullest benefit. Some are just rejecting it outright. Enough is enough, they holler.

• Telephones demonstrate just what technology overload is like.

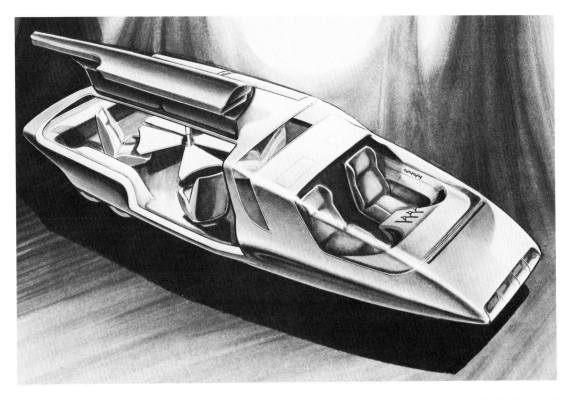

So many possibilities brought about by options. *Put that call on hold; pull this one out of memory...Oops! That was the pager. Where did I put that last call? And what is this blinking red light?* Camcorders were supposed to make home movies a lot easier. Seen one lately? People got tired of trying to figure them out. Program the VCR from the remote control? Forget it. Even children, brought up in the midst of this revolution cannot keep up.

Will technology get friendlier?

• I think I see a new trend starting to emerge. It is the era of simplicity. Technology will become kinder, friendlier and hidden. Once we wanted to see every little layer of switches. We wanted to operate buttons, turn knobs, dial in. Now we just want to be left alone.

• What gives me hope and support for my premise is a new product called the Gemstar VCR Plus. This looks like a remote control that eliminates the need to program your VCR when recording a television show. By punching in the proper code, published in your newspaper's television listings, it automatically sets the VCR for the right day and time. You won't have to drop the control panel and confront all of those meters, dials, switches and timers.

• What are the implications of this phenomenon for design?

DESIGN
Challenge

SCULPTURE SITE PLAN

A generous and wealthy person has offered to give your town a magnificent 22-foot tall sculpture for permanent display. There is some land available at the town park for an area to be set aside for the sculpture. As the town planner, your role is to design a space to reveal the sculpture, to provide a meditative setting for it, and to allow people to move freely around the work. You have a space of 600 square feet for the artwork. The ground slopes along a mild grade. You have complete freedom in the choice of materials for a platform, walls, overhangs, site furniture, and lighting.

Drama is the most important consideration, of course. Just think of the last horror movie you saw. When something or someone pops out from behind the door - that's drama. To invite the public in towards the sculpture is dramatic; to publicize it from 400 yards away is not. You want to entice people in and to draw them towards the art work. How will you accomplish this?

Here are some hints. Think about walls and wall heights; about entryways and exits; about bends and breaks and height changes; about landscaping. Maybe you want to give the viewers a little peek if they approach the sculpture from the right angle. How about a slit between two barriers? Maybe a piece of the sculpture could stick up above a barrier? Once people are near the sculpture, how will you guide them around it? Will you invite them to sit for a while or do you want them to move out quickly? Should there be a distinct entrance and exit zone, area or passageway? A festive arch or pavilion might be appropriate.

In order to convince the town board of your design, a site plan must be created. This should be in two scales. One will illustrate the placement of the whole sculpture area within the town park; the other will be of the sculpture area itself, in some detail. Once the drawings are completed you can add landscaping and parking to your scale model.

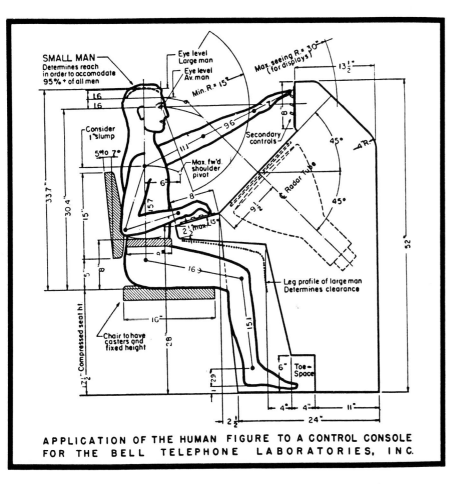

APPLICATION OF THE HUMAN FIGURE TO A CONTROL CONSOLE
FOR THE BELL TELEPHONE LABORATORIES, INC.

Ergonomics is the study of how technology can be designed to fit people. This was done by Henry Dreyfuss.

Humanizing technology

• I believe we must meet the challenge of humanizing technology. Our capacity to deal with tasks is limited. We expect technology not to just enrich our lives but to simplify them. As we become more and more unwilling to adjust to engineering, designers will have to adjust the engineering to us. It's here, at the point of the human-machine interface, that designers, whether in architecture, product or graphic practice will demonstrate their power to make our creations more humane and accessible.

• A practicing designer, or a student entering the field, must focus on the issues of the future while keeping an eye out to the past. Certainly environmental concerns are significant. Making technology "user-friendly" is a vital consideration. Your only limitations are the size of your imagination and a commitment to succeed.

• As the industrial revolution, the age of enlightenment and our information society blend together, it is the designer who will be at center stage. It is the designer who will clarify, humanize and beautify the human-made environment.